BOO

Second Edition

Newcomer's Guide to Canada
Revised and Updated

By Barbara Dixon
Diversity ERAA Training

COPYRIGHT © 2015 BY BARBARA DIXON, DIVERSITY ERAA TRAINING, WINNIPEG, MANITOBA, CANADA.

All rights reserved. No part of this book may be reprinted or reproduced in any form or by any electronic, mechanical or other means, now known or hereafter invented, including photocopying, recording and information storage and retrieval, without permission in writing from the author.

ISBN-13: 978-1514845226
ISBN -10: 1515845229

INTRODUCTION

This *Newcomer's Guide to Canada* was prepared to help new immigrants plan for their immigration journey and be prepared to become successful in Canada. There is an abundance of websites that provide excellent information to newcomers. Finding and reading all this information can be overwhelming.

Diversity ERAA Training's Newcomer's Guide tries to highlight the most important information newcomers need to know before they arrive in Canada and what they need to know once they arrive.

The *Newcomer's Guide to Canada* is divided into four chapters:
    Chapter 1: Pre-Arrival – Learning about Canada
    Chapter 2: Stages of Integration
    Chapter 3: Settlement and Integration
    Chapter 4: Finding a Job
    Chapter 5: Cultural Differences

Diversity ERAA Training provides integration assistance and job search mentoring to newcomers as well as diversity training for employers and professional sector groups.

If you are interested in having a Personalized Integration Plan (PIP) developed especially for you that provides websites to research customized to your profession and the city and province you hope to immigrate to, contact Diversity ERAA Training:
http://diversityeraa.ca

I hope you will find this *Guide* helpful!

Barbara Dixon
Senior Consultant and President, Diversity ERAA Training
Winnipeg, Manitoba, Canada

CONTENTS

CHAPTER 1: PRE-ARRIVAL

Learn About Canada	1
Canadian Cities Compared	12
Comparing Canada's Population and Age	15
Weather	16
Official Languages	22
Banking	23
Currency	25
Credit	26
Housing	26
Garbage Collection and Littering	29
Education	31
Canadian Laws	34
Transportation	36
Lesbian, Gay, Bi-Sexual, Transgendered, Two Spirit	36
Recreation and Leisure	37
Pre-Arrival Checklist	39

CHAPTER 2: STAGES OF INTEGRATION

Stages of Integration	41
Post-Traumatic Stress Disorder (PTSD)	43
Symptoms Checklist	44

CHAPTER 3: SETTLEMENT AND INTEGRATION

Settlement	47
Your First Week	47
Your First Few Weeks	54
Your First Year	58
Settlement and Integration Checklist	65

CHAPTER 4: FINDING A JOB

Preparing to Find a Job	67
Getting a License to Practice Your Profession	67
Transferable Skills	69
Transferable Skills Inventory	70
Alternative Career	76
Finding a Job	77
Workplace Communication Skills	79
Networking	81
Elevator Pitch	84
Canadian Work Experience	85
Mentorship	86
Writing Cover Letters	87
Resume (CV) Writing	89
Job Interview Preparation	90
Job Offer	93
Deductions from Your Paycheque	94
Employees' Rights	95
Finding a Job Checklist	98

CHAPTER 5: CULTURAL DIFFERENCES

Cultural Quiz	99
Perceptions and Assumptions	102
Cultural Values and Beliefs	102
Common Cultural Differences and Business Practices	104
Learning to Understand other Cultures	116
Discrimination and Racism	117
In Conclusion	118
Appendices	120
Bibliography	151
Index	156
About the Author	160

CHAPTER 1: PRE-ARRIVAL

Challenges and opportunities lie ahead when you arrive in Canada.

As a Permanent Resident of Canada, you have the same rights of mobility as Canadians. What this means is that you can move to wherever you want to live or where you find a job.

This section is designed to help ease the transition of moving to Canada.

Learn About Canada

Canada is a very large country. There are ten provinces and three territories. There are six time zones. Canada is much more than Toronto, Vancouver or Montreal. Have you ever heard of Winnipeg, Saskatoon, Edmonton, Ottawa or Halifax? These are just some of the other major cities, which you could choose to live in.

Large cities may have a surplus of labour and a shortage of jobs. Do your research. Remember to choose a destination where jobs exist in your field and where the cost of living is affordable to you.

Canada's West Coast Province: British Columbia

British Columbia is Canada's westernmost province and is set between the Pacific Ocean in the west and the province of Alberta and the Rocky Mountains in the east. According to Statistics Canada, 17.6% of Canada's immigrants live in British Columbia.[1]

---

[1] Statistics Canada, http://www12.statcan.gc.ca/nhs-enm/2011/as-sa/99-010-x/99-010-x2011001-eng.cfm

The cost of living in British Columbia depends on where you choose to live.

The capital of British Columbia is Victoria. It is located on the southern tip of Vancouver Island. Victoria is a medium-sized city. A high proportion of the labour force works in public administration, tourism and retail trade.[2] Victoria has pleasant weather, particularly during winter and has become a popular retirement destination. Local purchasing power in Victoria is 6.59% lower than in Toronto.[3]

For many newcomers, the only city they know of in British Columbia is Vancouver. Vancouver is Canada's 8th largest city. Major economic sectors include film, international commerce and trade, natural resources, technology and tourism.[4] Local purchasing power in Vancouver is 13.45% lower than in Toronto.[5]

Vancouver is the most expensive city in Canada to live. Demographia International Housing Affordability 2015 Survey ranked Vancouver as the second most unaffordable housing market in the world after Hong Kong.[6] Choosing to live in a different city or a smaller community in British Columbia will offer you a lower cost of living.

---

[2] Work BC, https://www.workbc.ca/Statistics/Labour-Market.aspx
[3] Numbeo, http://www.numbeo.com/cost-of-living/compare_cities.jsp?country1=Canada&country2=Canada&city1=Toronto&city2=Victoria

[4] Ibid
[5] Numbeo, http://www.numbeo.com/cost-of-living/compare_cities.jsp?country1=Canada&country2=Canada&city1=Toronto&city2=Vancouver

[6] 11th Annual Demographia International Housing Affordability Survey: 2015, http://www.demographia.com/dhi.pdf

Other cities to consider living in British Columbia include: Armstrong, Burnaby, Campbell River, Castlegar, Chilliwack, Colwood, Coquitlam, Courtenay, Cranbrook, Dawson Creek, Enderby, Fernie, Fort St. John, Grand Forks, Kamloops, Kelowna, Kimberley, Langford, Langley, Maple Ridge, Merritt, Nanaimo, Nelson, New Westminster, North Vancouver, Parksville, Penticton, Pitt Meadows, Port Alberni, Port Coquitlam, Port moody, Powell River, Prince George, Prince Rupert, Quesnel, Revelstoke, Richmond, Rossland, Salmon Arm, Surrey, Terrace, Trail, Vernon, White Rock and Williams Lake.

British Columbia is expected to be the fastest growing economy in Canada in 2016 due to the strong construction and housing sectors.

Immigration Portal for British Columbia:
www.welcomebc.ca/home.aspx

Canada's Prairie Provinces: Alberta, Saskatchewan and Manitoba

The three Prairie Provinces from west to east are: Alberta, Saskatchewan and Manitoba. According to Statistics Canada, 9.5% of Canada's immigrants live in Alberta, 5.0% in Manitoba and 2.3% in Saskatchewan. [7]

Alberta

Alberta's capital is Edmonton. Edmonton is Canada's 5th largest city. Finance, real estate, trade, professional, technical and management services and manufacturing are primary industries in Edmonton. [8]

---

[7] Ibid
[8] The City of Edmonton,
http://www.edmonton.ca/business_economy/demographics_profiles/industries.aspx

In 2015, Edmonton was named the 6th best large city to live in Canada.[9] Local purchasing power in Edmonton is 3.56% lower than in Toronto.[10]

Calgary is Canada's 3rd largest city by both population and area. In 2015, Calgary was named the 3rd best large city to live in Canada by MoneySense.[11] Calgary is the major centre for the global energy industry. Other prospective employers exist in the technology sector, finance and business services, manufacturing, transportation and logistics, film and creative industries.[12] Local purchasing power in Calgary is 13.11% higher than in Toronto. [13]

Brooks is Alberta's smallest city by area and Lacombe is the smallest city by population. Other cities to consider living in Alberta include: Airdrie, Camrose, Cherstermere, Cold Lake, Fort Saskatchewan, Grande Prairie, Leduc, Lethbridge, Lloydminster, Medicine Hat, red deer, Spruce Grove, St. Albert and Wetaskiwin.

Alberta has many cost of living advantages compared to the average cost of living in Canada. It is the only province in Canada with no provincial sales tax, the lowest tax on gasoline, and it has some of the lowest property taxes in the country.

Immigration Portal for Alberta:
http://albertacanada.com

---

[9] MoneySense, http://www.moneysense.ca/canadas-best-places-to-live-2015-full-ranking/
[10] Numbeo, , http://www.numbeo.com/cost-of-living/compare_cities.jsp?country1=Canada&city1=Toronto&country2=Canada&city2=Edmonton

[11] MoneySense, http://www.moneysense.ca/canadas-best-places-to-live-2015-full-ranking/
[12] Calgary Economic Development, http://www.calgaryeconomicdevelopment.com/industries
[13] Numbeo, http://www.numbeo.com/cost-of-living/compare_cities.jsp?country1=Canada&country2=Canada&city1=Toronto&city2=Calgary

Saskatchewan

Saskatchewan's capital is Regina. Regina is the 2nd largest city in Saskatchewan. Regina is the finance and insurance centre for Saskatchewan. Steel and manufacturing, information technology, energy and environment, finance, insurance and real estate, public administration and agribusiness are some other major industries in Regina. Local purchasing power in Regina is 5.91% higher than in Toronto.[14]

Saskatoon is Saskatchewan's largest city by both population and area. It is considered to be a medium-sized city and is one Canada's fastest growing cities. Primary industries include agriculture, mining, oil and gas, transportation and logistics. Local purchasing power in Saskatoon is 20.72% lower than in Toronto.[15]

Martensville is Saskatchewan's smallest city by area and Melville is smallest by population. Other cities to consider living in Saskatchewan include: Estevan, Flin Flon, Humboldt, Lloydminster, Meadow Lake, Melfort, Moose Jaw, North Battleford, Prince Albert, Swift Current, Warman, Weyburn and Yorkton.

The cost of living in Saskatchewan is considered low compared to the rest of Canada. The provincial sales tax is 5% and is the lowest of the nine provinces that charge a sales tax. Housing costs are lower in Saskatchewan than in most major cities in Canada making it affordable to own a home.

Immigration Portal Saskatchewan:
http://www.economy.gov.sk.ca/immigration/

---

[14] Numbeo, http://www.numbeo.com/cost-of-living/compare_cities.jsp?country1=Canada&country2=Canada&city1=Toronto&city2=Regina
[15] Numbeo, http://www.numbeo.com/cost-of-living/compare_cities.jsp?country1=Canada&country2=Canada&city1=Toronto&city2=Saskatoon

Manitoba

Manitoba's capital is Winnipeg. It is Canada's 7th largest city and Manitoba's largest city. It is considered to be a medium-sized city.

In 2015, Winnipeg was named the 4th best large city to live in Canada.[16] Sales and service, business, finance and administration, medical research, and logistics, trade and transportation are the major industries with employment.[17] Local purchasing power in Winnipeg is 6.81% lower than in Toronto.[18]

Brandon is the 2nd largest city in Manitoba. The majority of employment in Brandon is in the health care, social services, manufacturing and retail trade.[19]

Dauphin is Manitoba's smallest city by area and Flin Flon is smallest by population. Other cities to consider living in Manitoba include: Morden, Portage la Prairie, Selkirk, Steinbach, Thompson and Winkler.

Manitoba is one of the most affordable provinces in Canada. House prices, car insurance, utilities, and post-secondary tuition costs are some of the lowest costs in Canada. Manitoba continually has one of the lowest unemployment rates in Canada.

---

[16] MoneySense, http://www.moneysense.ca/canadas-best-places-to-live-2015-full-ranking/
[17] http://www.city-data.com/canada/Winnipeg-work.html
[18] Numbeo, http://www.numbeo.com/cost-of-living/compare_cities.jsp?country1=Canada&country2=Canada&city1=Toronto&city2=Winnipeg

[19] Economic Development Brandon, http://economicdevelopmentbrandon.com/industry-employment-business

According to the Conference Board of Canada, Manitoba is primed to be among Canada's leaders in economic growth in the next two years. Manitoba is expected to have the second-fastest growing economy in 2016 and it is forecast to be even stronger in 2017 due to the strong construction, manufacturing and service sectors.[20]

Immigration Portal for Manitoba:
www.immigratemanitoba.com

Central Canada: Ontario and Quebec

Central Canada refers to Canada's two largest and most populous provinces, Ontario and Quebec. According to Statistics Canada, 53.3% of Canada's immigrants live in Ontario and 14.4% of Canada's immigrants live in Quebec.[21]

> **When you are choosing a place to live in Canada, it is important to learn about all the different regions, cities, job opportunities and the cost of living.**

Ontario

Ontario's capital and Canada's largest city is Toronto. The key industry sectors are business and professional services, design, education, fashion, film and television, finance environmental, life sciences, music, tourism and hospitality, and technology.[22]

---

[20] Provincial Outlook executive Summary: autumn 2015, The Conference Board of Canada, December 7, 2015, http://www.conferenceboard.ca/e-library/abstract.aspx?did=7557
[21] Statistics Canada, http://www12.statcan.gc.ca/nhs-enm/2011/as-sa/99-010-x/99-010-x2011001-eng.cfm
[22] City of Toronto, *Key Industry Sectors*, http://www1.toronto.ca/wps/portal/contentonly?vgnextoid=401132d0b6d1e310VgnVCM10000071d60f89RCRD

Ottawa is Canada's capital and 4th largest city. It is a medium-sized city. In 2015, Ottawa was named the best large city in Canada to live.[23] Public administration and high technology are the primary sectors in Ottawa.[24] Local purchasing power in Ottawa is 0.16% lower than Toronto.[25]

Mississauga is Canada's 6th largest city. Brampton is Canada's 9th largest city and Hamilton is Canada's 10th largest city. Hamilton, Kitchener, London, Oshawa, St. Catherines, Windsor and Sudbury are all considered to be medium-sized cities.

Other cities to consider living in Ontario include: Barrie, Belleville, Brampton, Brant, Brantford, Brockville, Burlington, Cambridge, Clarence-Rockland, Cornwall, Elliot Lake, Guelph, Haldimand County, Kawartha Lakes, Kenora, Kingston, Kitchener, London, Markham, Niagara Falls, Norfolk County, North Bay, Orillia, Oshawa, Owen Sound, Peterborough, Pickering, Port Colbourne, Prince Edward County, Quinte West, Sarnia, Sault Ste. Marie, St. Catherines, St. Thomas, Stratford, Temiskaming Shores, Thorold, Thunder Bay, Timmins, Vaughan, Waterloo, Welland, Windsor and Woodstock.

Immigration Portal for Ontario:
www.ontarioimmigration.ca

Quebec

Quebec's capital is Quebec City. It is Quebec's 2nd largest city and was ranked in 2015 as the 2nd best large city to live in.[26]

---

[23] MoneySense, http://www.moneysense.ca/canadas-best-places-to-live-2015-full-ranking/

[24] City of Ottawa, *Economy and Demographics*, http://ottawa.ca/en/long-range-financial-plans/long-range-financial-plan-iii-part-1-and-part-2/economy-and-demographics

[25] Numbeo, Numbeo, http://www.numbeo.com/cost-of-living/compare_cities.jsp?country1=Canada&country2=Canada&city1=Toronto&city2=Ottawa

[26] MoneySense, http://www.moneysense.ca/canadas-best-places-to-live-2015-full-ranking/

Montreal is Canada's 2nd largest city and Quebec's largest city by population.

The key industries in Quebec are ICT and electronics, life sciences, food processing, insurance and financial services, green and smart building and value-added materials and transportation equipment.[27]

Immigration Portal for Quebec:
http://www.immigration-quebec.gouv.qc.ca/fr/index.php

Atlantic Provinces: New Brunswick, Nova Scotia, Prince Edward Island and Newfoundland and Labrador

Canada's Atlantic provinces from west to east include: New Brunswick, Nova Scotia, Prince Edward Island and Newfoundland and Labrador. According to Statistics Canada, 0.5% of Canadian immigrants live in New Brunswick, 0.9% live in Nova Scotia, 0.2% live in Prince Edward Island and 0.2% live in Newfoundland and Labrador.[28]

New Brunswick

New Brunswick is Canada's only official bilingual (French and English) province. The three biggest cities in New Brunswick are Fredericton, Moncton and Saint John.

---

[27] Quebec International, http://www.quebecinternational.ca/key-industries
[28] Statistics Canada, http://www12.statcan.gc.ca/nhs-enm/2011/as-sa/99-010-x/99-010-x2011001-eng.cfm

The capital city of New Brunswick is Fredericton. Major industries in Fredericton include public administration, education, information technology, engineering and environmental technologies.[29]

Saint John is New Brunswick's largest city by population and area. The major industries include oil and gas, transport/distribution, electricity, brewing and call centres.[30] Moncton is a growing high technology and service industry city.[31]

Immigration Portal for New Brunswick:
www.gnb.ca/Immigration

Nova Scotia

The capital of Nova Scotia is Halifax. Halifax is the largest municipality city by area in Nova Scotia. Halifax harbor is the world's 2nd largest harbor. The major industries in Halifax include aerospace, health care, education, skilled trades and digital industries.[32] Local purchasing power in Halifax is 9.872% lower than in Toronto.[33]

Immigration Portal for Nova Scotia:
www.novascotiaimmigration.ca

---

[29] City of Fredericton, http://www.fredericton.ca/en/communityculture/communityprofile.asp
[30] http://foundlocally.com/stjohns/Local/Info-CityInfo.htm
[31] Living in Canada, living in New Brunswick, http://www.livingin-canada.com/living-in-new-brunswick.html
[32] http://twosmallmen.com/halifax-ns-movers/main-industries-and-job-opportunities-in-halifax
[33] Numbeo, http://www.numbeo.com/cost-of-living/compare_cities.jsp?country1=Canada&country2=Canada&city1=Toronto&city2=Halifax

Prince Edward Island

Prince Edward Island is Canada's smallest province. Its capital is Charlottetown. The main employers in Charlottetown are in sales and service occupations, business, finance and administration and trades.[34] Summerside is the other city in Prince Edward Island.

Immigration Portal for Prince Edward Island: www.gov.pe.ca/immigration

Newfoundland and Labrador

Newfoundland and Labrador is the 16th largest island in the world. The capital of Newfoundland and Labrador is St. John's, a medium-sized city.

St. John's is the largest city in Newfoundland and Labrador. Industry sectors include oil and gas, hydro, ocean technology, construction, education, culture and tourism.[35] Local purchasing power in St. John's is 30.65% lower than in Toronto.[36]

Immigration Portal for Newfoundland and Labrador: www.nlimmigration.ca

---

[34] http://www.city-data.com/canada/Charlottetown-City-work.html
[35] The Canadian Trade Commissioner Service, *St. John's: An Emerging Economy and Cultural Capital*, http://www.international.gc.ca/investors-investisseurs/cities-villes/saint_johns.aspx?lang=eng
[36] Numbeo, http://www.numbeo.com/cost-of-living/compare_cities.jsp?country1=Canada&country2=Canada&city1=Toronto&city2=St.+John%27s%2C+NL

Northern Territories: Yukon, Northwest Territories and Nunavut

Canada has three northern territories: Yukon, Northwest Territories and Nunavut. The capital city of Yukon is Whitehorse. The capital of Northwest Territories is Yellowknife. The capital of Nunavut is Iqaluit.

Immigration Portal for Yukon: www.immigration.gov.yk.ca

Immigration Portal for Northwest Territories: www.gov.nt.ca

Immigration Portal for Nunavut: www.gov.nu.ca

Canadian Cities Compared

According to the 2011 National Household Survey, Canada's foreign-born population was 6.8 million.[37] This means that one in every five people living in Canada is an immigrant.

Cities in Canada vary in size and population. You want to choose a place to live where you can use your work skills and where you will have the lifestyle you want.

Canada's largest cities include: Toronto, Montreal and Vancouver.

Why do many immigrants choose Toronto and Vancouver as their destination? Have you ever thought about this?

Ask yourself if someone were immigrating to your country, where would they plan to live?

---

[37] Statistics Canada, *Immigration and Ethnocultural Diversity in Canada*, http://www12.statcan.gc.ca/nhs-enm/2011/as-sa/99-010-x/99-010-x2011001-eng.cfm

Most likely, it would be a place they had heard of or visited. This is the same reason many immigrants choose Toronto and Vancouver. They have heard of these two cities and may not know much about the rest of Canada.

City	Vancouver	Edmonton	Winnipeg	Toronto
Pop (2014)[38]	2.5 million	1.3 million	770 thousand	6 million
Foreign Born[39]	40.0%	20.4%	20.6%	46.0%
Unemployment (2015)	5.9%[40]	6.2%[41]	5.8%[42]	7.1%[43]
Median Income (2013)[44]	$73,390	$98,480	$77,770	$72,830
Average House Price (2015)[45]	$947,334	$371,756	$271,759	$630,876

You can see, that the cost of housing in Toronto and Vancouver is much higher than other cities. If you want to purchase a house in Canada versus rent an apartment, this is something to consider.

---

[38] Statistics Canada, http://www.statcan.gc.ca/tables-tableaux/sum-som/l01/cst01/demo05a-eng.htm
[39] Statistics Canada, http://www12.statcan.gc.ca/nhs-enm/2011/as-sa/fogs-spg/Pages/CMACASelector.cfm?lang=E&level=3
[40] Employment and Social Development Canada, http://srv129.services.gc.ca/ei_regions/eng/vancouv.aspx?rates=1
[41] Employment and Social Development Canada, http://srv129.services.gc.ca/ei_regions/eng/edmonton.aspx?rates=1
[42] Employment and Social Development Canada, http://srv129.services.gc.ca/ei_regions/eng/winnipeg.aspx?rates=1
[43] Employment and Social Development Canada, http://srv129.services.gc.ca/ei_regions/eng/toronto.aspx?rates=1
[44] Statistics Canada, *Median Total Income, by Family Type, By Census Metropolitan Areas*, http://www.statcan.gc.ca/tables-tableaux/sum-som/l01/cst01/famil107a-eng.htm
[45] The Canadian Real Estate Association, *National Average Price Map*, http://crea.ca/content/national-average-price-map

Do not just choose a place based on a higher income because this often means the cost of living is also higher.

There are many other cities and towns to choose to live in Canada. Do not make the mistake of just choosing a place you have heard of in Canada. Keep your options open.

Medium-sized cities include: Victoria, Edmonton, Calgary, Saskatoon, Regina, Winnipeg, Sudbury, Windsor, London, Kitchener, St. Catherines, Hamilton, Oshawa, Quebec City, Halifax and St. John's.

Small-sized cities include: Kelowna, Red Deer, Moose Jaw, Brandon, Moncton, Sydney, Charlottetown and Corner Brook.

Canada is a very large country. There are many towns of various sizes and rural areas where you can also choose to live.

Look at a map of Canada. Do research to find out about the geography of the different areas. Find out where jobs in your profession exist.

Do not just automatically choose what you know. Explore the different regions of Canada to see what suits the lifestyle you want when you live here.

Comparing Canada's Population and Age[46]

	Canada	China	India	Nigeria	Philippines
Pop.	35 million	1.4 billion	1.2 billion	177 million	92.3 million
Land Area	9,984,670 km²	9,596,960 km²	3,287,263 km²	300,000 km²	796,095 km²
Pop. Density	4 people per km²	145 people per km²	421 people per km²	330 people per km²	236 people per km²
Median Age	41.7 years	36.7 years	27 years	23.5 years	22.6 years

When you compare landmass, the Philippines is only 3% the size of Canada, India is 323% the size of Canada and Nigeria is 9% the size of Canada.

What does this mean for you as a newcomer?

Most people live in the southern part of Canada. Even knowing this, you have a very large area from which to choose from in terms of where you want to live. Conduct research to find the best place for you.

You will notice that there are not as many people. Initially, for some of you, this might make you feel lonely. For some, you will immediately enjoy being in a less crowded place.

---

[46] https://www.cia.gov **and** http://data.worldbank.org/indicator/SP.POP.TOTL

Given Canada's aging population, your children and you will have job opportunities as the Canadian workforce retires.

Weather

Canada has four seasons: Autumn/Fall (starts September 21), Winter (starts December 21), Spring (starts March 21) and Summer (starts June 21).

Winter officially lasts three months, but in reality, depending on where you live in Canada, is about 5 months long. Most newcomers worry about how they will adjust to the cold weather.

Your first winter will be your worst and your best. Most of you have never experienced the freezing temperatures that exist in Canada during winter. The key to enjoying winter is to stay active and wear the appropriate clothing.

All buildings and vehicles are heated during the winter. You will be warm when you are indoors. However, it is extremely important that you stay active and get outside during the winter. Otherwise, you can become depressed and isolated.

Learn how to ice skate or snowboard or ski or join a curling team. Take your children tobogganing (a sled that you sit on and go down a hill).

Winter

Summer

It is also important to maintain adequate levels of Vitamin D during winter months due to the lack of exposure to sunshine. From September 1 to June 30, you should take a minimum of 1000 International Units (IU) daily. Ask your doctor for the recommended dosage for you.

Dressing appropriately for the weather is extremely important! Your skin can freeze depending on the temperature and wind chill.

Here are some tips on how to dress in winter.

Layer your Clothes

The best way to keep warm during winter is to layer your clothes. Start with a base, such as long underwear (sometimes referred to as long johns) or leggings and then add a few mid-layers topped with a wind-proof shell. Buy a coat that falls below the waist, preferably between your bottom and your knees. Pay the extra money to buy a good pair of winter boots. Add more layers depending on the outdoor activity.

When buying winter clothes, look for warm materials such as wool, fleece or thick synthetics. For coats, look for thinsulate or down linings. Avoid wearing cotton in winter as it can draw heat away from your body. Remember that loose clothing provides more insulation.

> ### Remember to Cover Your Head, Ears, Neck, Hands and Feet

It is extremely important to cover your head, ears, neck, hands and feet during winter. These extremities can easily become frostbitten (injured by freezing or partial freezing). It is also very important to keep from getting wet during winter. So for example, if your children are playing in the snow, they may need to change their mittens once they get wet.

Head and Ears

In cold weather, we lose most of our body heat through our heads. Wear a wool hat or toque that covers your ears. In Canada, a toque (pronounced tuke) is another way of saying winter hat.

Neck

Buy and wear scarves that are woolen, thick and broad. You can use scarves to cover your small children's nose, mouth and top of forehead when they are playing outside.

Hands

Wear gloves or mittens that are made of wool or are insulated and covered with leather.

Feet

Buy a good pair of boots that are temperature rated and have a good grip on the bottom. Good quality boots costs approximately $200 for adults and about $80 for children. As you get accustomed to winter, you can then buy fashion boots. Wear winter socks that are made of wool or fleece. Be careful that your feet are comfortable in your boots and that the circulation is not constricted.

Winter can be fun if you are prepared and dress for it. Go outside! Learn to skate or ski or snowboard.

> Explore winter and all its wonders!

Understand Wind Chill

In Canada, weather is a daily topic of conversation. People will check the weather forecast several times a day as the weather can change dramatically.

In the winter, you need to understand Canada's Wind Chill Index. The Wind Chill Index equates outdoor conditions to an equivalent temperature with no wind. It tells you the degree of chill that your skin senses. By understanding the wind chill index, you can avoid injuries from the cold.

Wind Speed (km/hr)	Temperature (Celsius)								
0	0	-5	-10	-15	-20	-25	-30	-35	-40	-45
10	-3	-9	-15	-21	-27	-33	-39	-45	-51	-57
20	-5	-12	-18	-24	-30	-37	-43	-49	-56	-62
30	-6	-13	-20	-26	-33	-39	-45	-52	-59	-65

Wind Speed (km/hr)	Temperature (Celsius)								
40	-7	-14	-21	-27	-34	-41	-48	-54	-61	-68
50	-8	-15	-22	-29	-35	-42	-49	-56	-63	-69
60	-9	-16	-23	30	-36	-43	-50	-57	-64	-71

Source: http://www.almanac.com/content/windchill-chart-canada

When the wind chill goes below -27C, there is a risk of frostbite. What this means is that exposed skin can freeze in 10-30 minutes.

Find out the weather forecast on radio or television, in newspapers or on-line at Environment Canada before dressing to go outside.

Official Languages

Canada has two official languages: English and French. Depending on where you live in Canada, you may need to improve your English or French skills.

Free language training classes are offered across Canada. Your sponsor or settlement counselor will be able to direct you for language testing.

Learning another language is always of benefit and classes are offered if you want to improve your language skills or learn another language.

Banking

Financial institutions in Canada are secure. You can feel safe keeping your money in a Canadian bank or credit union.

> **If a Canadian bank exists in your country, you can open a bank account before you arrive**

Both banks and credit unions offer residential mortgage financing, consumer credit and deposit services, terms deposits, Registered Retirement Savings Plans (RRSPs), Registered Retirement Income Funds (RRIFs), business products, loans, financial counseling, trust and insurance services.

Canada has a national system of banking. This means that no matter where you live in Canada, you can access similar services at the same price at any bank. Shareholders own banks. There are 29 domestic banks, 24 foreign bank subsidiaries and 27 full-service foreign bank branches.[47]

The five major banks in Canada include: Canadian Imperial Bank of Commerce (CIBC), Bank of Montreal (BMO), Bank of Nova Scotia (Scotiabank), Toronto Dominion Bank of Canada (TD) and Royal Bank of Canada (RBC). Other banking institutions also exist in Canada.

---

[47] Office of the Superintendent of Financial Institutions, May 2014, http://www.osfi-bsif.gc.ca/eng/pages/default.aspx

Anyone can open a bank or credit union account in Canada if they provide the required identification. You do not need to have a job or money to deposit to open an account.

BMO	CIBC	RBC	SCOTIABANK	TD BANK
Australia Brazil China India Ireland Mexico Switzerland Taiwan United Kingdom United States	Asia Australia Brazil Caribbean China India United Kingdom United States	Asia Caribbean Europe Middle East United Kingdom United States	Asia Caribbean Central America Latin America Mexico United States	Asia Europe United States

Credit unions are owned and controlled by their members. The cost of becoming a member ranges from $5 to $125.

There are approximately 700 different credit unions (caisses populaires in Quebec) in Canada. Credit Unions often offer better value than banks, particularly with competitive and transparent pricing on mortgages.

Bank and credit union debit cards can be used at any ATM across the country 24 hours a day, seven days a week. You can also set up your account to have Internet and/or telephone banking.

Many employers pay their employees through direct deposit. This means you will need a bank or credit union account for your employer to deposit your earnings.

Currency

5 cents is called a nickel

10 cents is called a dime

25 cents is called a quarter

1 dollar is called a loonie

2 dollars is called a toonie

Paper money comes in denominations of $5, $10, $20, $50 and $100

It will take you some time before you are comfortable knowing what Canadian currency is worth. Try not to convert from your money, i.e., rupees, to Canadian dollars. It is best to learn the currency and what it is worth in terms of what it costs to live in Canada and what you can afford to spend.

While you are getting accustomed to the currency, make a monthly budget of your expenditures. Try to stay on budget and not go into debt.

Credit

In Canada, you can apply for one or more credit cards. Credit cards are available from banks and credit unions plus large stores.

Credit means that you borrow money to purchase something now and pay it back later with interest. Interest is the fee that you are charged to borrow the money. Interest rates vary from credit cards to credit card, so it is important to get a credit card with the lowest interest rate possible.

It is extremely important to maintain your credit rating in Canada. Make sure to pay at least the minimum owing each month as shown on your bill. If you can, the best is to pay your bill in full each month.

> **You need to maintain a good credit rating in order to get loans to purchase large items like a home or car.**

Housing

When you come to Canada, you will need housing. Most newcomers initially rent rather than buy.

Here is information about the types of rental housing in Ca

- Rooms – a private bedroom in a large house with s kitchen and bathroom
- Apartments – A self-contained unit in a building
- Duplexes or triplexes – a house that is divided into two or three units
- Townhouse – Three or more units built side-by-side and share adjoining walls
- Single-family detached – a home that stands alone and sits on its own lot

Tenants have rights and responsibilities and are protected by the law. The tenant is responsible for paying the rent as scheduled, usually once per month. The tenant is responsible for keeping the rental unit clean and well maintained. Multiple families cannot use one apartment unit.

Landlords are the people who own the rental building. The landlord also has rights and responsibilities. The landlord is responsible for keeping the building in good repair and collecting rent. Landlords can raise rent once in a 12-month period. The provincial government determines rent increase amounts. The landlord cannot exceed the legal rental increase.

To find a place to rent, first determine the area you want to live in. Ask people about safe neighborhoods to live in. Then, check your local Kijiji website for rentals. Visit several different places before deciding which one to rent. Ask what your rent includes: heat, electricity, parking, water, cable and/or use of a gym or common area.

nce you decide on a place to rent, you will be asked to sign a lease. This is a written contract so be sure to read it before signing. You will also be asked for a security deposit to cover any damage that might happen while you are living in the rental unit. The law requires that your deposit include only the first and last month's rent.

> **Your housing costs should not exceed 30 - 32% of your gross household income.**

Source: Royal Bank of Canada

On the day you move in, check thoroughly and make note or take a photograph of any damage you find, such as carpet holes or stains, scratches on cupboards and/or water stains on ceilings. Ask the landlord to sign the list of damages and keep a copy for your records. You will get your security deposit returned when you vacate if there is no new damage.

When you want to move out of your rental unit, you must give your landlord prior written notice, at least one month or more depending on the province, before the first day of the month when you want to move out. You are also responsible for cleaning your apartment thoroughly once all your possessions are removed.

Many newcomers buy a home after a few years living in Canada. Again, the first step is to decide what neighborhoods you want to live in and what type of house you can afford.

There are different types of homes you can purchase:

- Condominium – Multi-unit buildings where you purchase a unit
- Semi-detached – Separate land and separate entrances with a common shared wall
- Townhouse – Attached side by side to a series of other homes
- Single Detached – Free-standing house where land and home are owned

Meet with a mortgage specialist at your financial institution who can help you determine what you can afford. They will explain that you need a down payment and will tell you the amount of mortgage you qualify for. Once you are pre-approved for a mortgage, then you can determine the size and features of the home you want to purchase. You will need an established, good credit rating to qualify for a mortgage.

Most homebuyers hire a real estate agent to help them purchase a home. Real estates do not cost the purchaser a fee. The home seller pays them. Real estate agents will show you different homes and help you get the best possible purchase price on the home you want to buy. They will assist you in making the official *Offer to Purchase*.

Garbage Collection and Littering

Canadian cities have garbage collection and recycling programs. Garbage is typically collected weekly. In smaller towns and rural areas, there are garbage dumps where you deliver your garbage.

It is illegal in Canada to litter. This means that you cannot throw garbage, waste materials or cigarettes on public or private property. You cannot throw it out of a car window. There are waste and recycling receptacles on major streets and parks.

Recycling is part of garbage collection for your household waste. Typically the following items can be recycled in your Blue Bin:

Plastic
- Plastic bottles and containers #1-7

Paper
- All paper and junk mail
- Milk and juice cartons
- Cardboard boxes
- Paperboard and frozen food boxes
- Newspapers, magazines and catalogues
- Paper bags, paper cups, empty pizza boxes

Glass
- Glass bottles and jars

Metal
- Metal cans, aluminum foil and trays

In some cities, fresh products are also recycled in a Green Bin. Typically the following items can be recycled in your Green Bin:

Food
- Meat, shellfish and fish products
- Dairy products and egg shells
- Coffee grounds, paper filters and tea bags
- Fruit and vegetable scraps
- Candies, cookies and cake
- Baking ingredients and herbs
- Bread, cereal and pasta

Paper
- Paper food packing such as ice cream boxes, flour and sugar bags, used paper towels, napkins and paper plates
- Diapers and sanitary products

Plants and Animal
- Household plants including soil
- Animal waste and cat litter
- Pet food

Check with your local area to see what is specifically accepted in the recycling program where you live.

Education

Education is a provincial and territorial responsibility and is publicly funded. All provinces require teachers to have a license or certificate to teach in public schools.

Publicly funded schools are free. All boys and girls between the ages of 5 or 6 and 16 or 18 must attend school depending on where you live. This is the law.

Children must go to school every day. If your child is absent due to illness or for personal reasons, you must tell the school.

> **Most Canadian children attend public NOT private schools**

There are different schools for different age groups: elementary (Kindergarten to Grade 5 or 6), middle (Grade 6 or 7 to Grade 8 or 9) and high school (Grade 9 or 10 to Grade 12). In most schools, boys and girls learn together in the same classroom. There are no school uniforms but most schools have a dress code.

Children go to school Monday to Friday during the school year, except for holidays. Schools operate from September to June and students attend between approximately 9 a.m. to 3:30 p.m. Summer vacation is during July and August. Winter vacation is between late December to early January. Spring vacation is sometime in March depending on the province.

Public schools tend to receive better funding and have more programming than privately funded schools.

There are also private and religious schools, which are outside the public funding. Private and religious schools must follow the same curriculum as publicly funded schools. Some private schools are for boys or girls only. There is a fee to send your child to a private or religious school.

There is also home schooling, where children receive their education at home taught by a parent or guardian. Home schooling must follow the same curriculum as publicly funded schools.

Students can attend English-language or French-language schooling. You may also have an option for your children to attend a language immersion school. Immersion programs are offered in many different languages. Check with your local school board to see what languages are offered.

Depending on how close you live to your child's school, your child can walk to school. Children who live too far from the school are bussed. School boards provide buses at minimal to no cost to you. Typically, once your child is 12 years old or in Grade 7, they are expected to take public transportation to school.

Children will get a report card several times during the school year that will tell you about their progress. Parents are encouraged to get involved with the school by meeting your child's teacher, attending parent-teacher meetings, school concerts and plays, and volunteering for events.

Differences in Education

Canadian students are under less pressure than students in some other countries.

You may or may not be used to the type of teaching style in Canada. In many countries, education tends to be teacher-centered whereas in Canada, education is student-centered. Canadian teachers use diversified teaching methods like group work, assignments, computer games and role-playing. There is not much, if any, time spent on lectures. Homework assignments are limited. Marks are not based solely on tests and examinations. Teachers supply handouts of many of the learning materials.

Students are expected to participate, use their imagination and creativity, and learn through discovery. You may have to help your child adjust to this new method of teaching and learning. You may have to also adjust as a parent because the system and expectations of teachers and students may be very different from what you are used to.

Choosing a Public School

If all teachers are certified and all schools follow the same provincial curriculum, how do you know the best schools for your children?

School choice varies according to city and province. For example, Manitoba parents can select any school in the province provided there are spaces available. In other places, children must attend the local neighborhood school. Consequently, where you select to live may determine where your children attend school.

Ask friends, relatives, acquaintances, mentors and co-workers for their opinions about what schools in your city are considered to be the best.

Canadian Laws

As a permanent resident or citizen of Canada, you are expected to understand and obey Canadian laws.

The police in Canada are not corrupt. They are safe and enforce the law. Do not offer money, gifts or services in exchange for special treatment. Offering bribes to anyone working in the legal system is illegal and you can get up to 14 years imprisonment.

You should call the police if you are a victim of a crime, see a crime taking place or know about criminal activities. In Canada, you are presumed innocent until proven guilty.

> **The emergency police telephone number in all parts of Canada is 911**

Family/Domestic Violence

Family violence is defined as different kinds of abuse that adults or children may have in their families. All kinds of physical and sexual abuse, including unwanted sexual activity with your husband or wife is considered illegal.

It is a crime to:
- Abuse a child by hitting them with an object, touching them sexually or forcing them into marriage
- Abuse a family member in a financial or psychological way
- Abuse or be cruel to an animal
- Beat, hit, kick or punch a family member including a child or spouse
- Have any sexual contact with a child
- Kill someone including honour killings
- Neglect a child by not providing adequate food, clothing and housing
- Perform female genital circumcision or
- Threaten to hurt someone

There are safe shelters for women and children who are abused. Counselling is also available.

> **Discipline of children in some countries is considered abuse in Canada.**
>
> **Victims of family violence should immediately call 911.**

Transportation

All cities and most major towns in Canada have a public transportation system with one or more modes of transportation such as a bus, subway, streetcar or light-rail train. In many cities and towns, there are also transportation services available specifically for people with limited mobility or a disability. You can get more information about public transportation in your city or town by calling a transit information line or visiting the website of your municipal government.

All cities and some towns have one or more companies that offer taxi service. Unlike in many countries, taxis in Canada are expensive. People tend to use them when they have no alternative. Taxis have automatic meters that use set rates to calculate the cost of your trip. The rates are fixed and cannot be negotiated. You pay the amount indicated on the meter at the end of the ride. Taxi drivers expect tips particularly if they have loaded your baggage into the trunk (boot) of their vehicle.

To get a taxi, you call the taxi company and they will pick you up at the address you provide. Alternatively, you can catch a taxi at a designated taxi stand such as the ones found at airports. You can try waving your hand at an empty taxi driving by you, but they may or may not stop to collect you.

Lesbian, Gay, Bi-Sexual, Transgendered, Two Spirit (LGBTT)

Canadians believe and value freedom from discrimination. This may be one of the reasons you are coming to Canada.

In Canada, everyone has the right to live their lives without being discriminated against for race, creed, ethnic background, political beliefs or sexual orientation.

In Canada, it is socially and legally acceptable to be gay or lesbian (homosexual), bi-sexual, transgendered or two spirit (an Indigenous person who identifies with both male and female gender roles). Gay and lesbian persons have the same rights and freedoms as all Canadians. They can get married, adopt children, and be on their same-sex spouse's medical and pension plans.

Recreation and Leisure

One of the many benefits of coming to Canada is that you will have more time to spend with your family. Most Canadian provinces have labour laws, which dictate the number of working hours per week. On average, most Canadians work 40 hours per week, 5 days per week.

Every province in Canada has beautiful landscapes for you to enjoy. Visit the many parks, go to the museums, historic sites and lakes, tour the art galleries and participate in activities at recreation facilities.

In Canada, both females and males play sports. During the winter, there is ice hockey, skating, snowboarding and curling plus indoor activities such as swimming, tennis, badminton, volleyball and basketball. During the warmer months, there are sports such as baseball, soccer, swimming and lacrosse. Both children and adults enjoy playing sports.

Most cities in Canada offer recreational programs. In some cities, these recreational programs are combined into a booklet called a *Leisure Guide*. You can usually find the *Leisure Guide* or recreational activities under the City's website. This is a good place to start to participate in Canadian recreational activities.

Pre-Arrival Document Checklist

Before you arrive in Canada, it is important to gather all the documents belonging to you and all your family members who are immigrating. Here is a checklist you can use to ensure you have all the documents you need to remember to bring.

Documents	☑
Birth Certificates and Passports	
Marriage or Divorce Certificate	
Death Certificate for Deceased Spouse	
Adoption Records for Adopted Children	
Educational Degrees, Diplomas and/or Certificates for University, College and High School	
Official Educational Transcripts With Courses Taken to Obtain Degree, Diploma and/or Certificate	
Official Vaccination Records	
Medical and Dental Records	
Driver's License and/or International Driving Permit	
Reference Letters from Past Employers	
Children's School and Vaccination Records	

CHAPTER 2: STAGES OF INTEGRATION

Stages of Integration

> **All newcomers go through all Stages of Integration**

Different family members go through each stage differently. This can cause friction in the family. For some unknown reason, children and women tend to adapt to the change quicker than men.

Be aware of, and sensitive to your moods and those of others in your family. Post a list of the different stages in a visible place to refer to so you can identify which stages everyone is in.

Here is a brief description of each stage:

Stage 1: Honeymoon

This stage usually occurs the first few days or weeks after arriving in Canada. You may be excited and eager. You feel confident and optimistic. When you arrive, everything is new and exciting. It is like being on a holiday where you are the tourist taking in everything and everyone.

Stage 2: Culture Shock

This stage usually occurs during the first 6 months in Canada. You start to feel frustrated, disappointed and overwhelmed. You miss your family and friends and feel lonely.

You start to focus on the differences between yourself and Canada mainly looking at the negative. You may have difficulty sleeping, be sad, homesick and/or exhausted. You may cry unexplainably. You may overeat or not feel like eating at all. You may be angry and lash out at family members. You may feel depressed and start to withdraw.

At this stage, you may dislike Canadian culture and Canadians. You may criticize, mock or show animosity towards Canadians.

Stage 3: Adjustment

You start to become more familiar and comfortable with the culture, people, food and language of Canada. You are less homesick and have started to make friends. You start to get involved in the community and feel more confident and in control. You regain your sense of humour. You now know how to better adapt to living in Canada.

Stage 4: Acceptance

At this stage, you feel comfortable in Canada, have made friends and are involved in the community. You are able to compare both the good and bad of Canada with the good and bad of your home country. You now know how things are done in Canada. You now start to view Canada as your second home.

Stage 5: Integration

At this stage you can now live comfortably in two cultures, your own and Canadian. You adopt certain behaviours from the new culture. You view yourself as a Canadian from (home country) rather than a (home country) living in Canada. You now feel "at home".

Post-Traumatic Stress Disorder (PTSD)

Some of you may have left your country due to war or persecution. Leaving your home for these reasons, may cause you to have a delayed response to the trauma or pressures you felt.

Are you having trouble sleeping? Do you have nightmares? Are you feeling lonely and depressed? Are you having an upset stomach or constant headaches?

If you answered yes to any of these questions, you could be suffering from Post-Traumatic Stress Disorder or PTSD. PTSD is a natural reaction to terrible experiences. As a refugee, you may have witnessed or experienced your friends and family members being tortured or killed. You and your family were forced to leave your home and as such, this would have been a traumatic event that could cause PTSD.

PTSD can affect anyone including children long after any real danger has passed. Symptoms can appear months to years after.

There is help in Canada for you if you are experiencing symptoms of PTSD or depression. Talk to your doctor, your settlement counselor or your sponsor. Contact the Canadian Mental Health Association who can direct you to help: **www.cmha.ca**

If you feel like you are suicidal, call 911 or go to your closest Emergency Department at your local hospital. If you need someone to talk with immediately, call your local crisis line. You can find crisis telephone lines at:
www.partnersformh.ca/resources/find-help/crisis-centres-across-canada/

Symptoms Checklist

Some Common Symptoms	
Adults	☑
Flashbacks of the traumatic event	☐
Nightmares	☐
Feeling emotionally numb	☐
Feeling strong guilt	☐
Feeling depressed	☐
Feeling excessively worried	☐
Difficulty sleeping	☐
Angry outbursts	☐
Feeling tense	☐
Loss of interest in activities you used to enjoy	☐
Fear someone may harm you	☐
Difficulty concentrating	☐
Drug or alcohol abuse	☐
Suicidal thoughts	☐

Pre-School Children	☐
Thumb-sucking or nail-biting	☐
Crying for no apparent reason	☐
Clinging to mother or caregiver	☐
Bedwetting	☐
Fear of dark or sleeping alone	☐
Children	☐
Anxious or depressed	☐
May refuse to go to school	☐
Stomachaches and/or headaches	☐
Re-enact or replay trauma	☐
Sleep disturbances including nightmares	☐
Angry outbursts	☐
Fear of dark	☐
Unable to concentrate	☐
Teenagers	☐
Risk-taking behaviours	☐
Difficulties in School	☐

Teenagers	☐
Is very self-conscious	☐
Becomes very rebellious	☐
Becomes withdrawn and depressed	☐
Sleep and eating disturbances	☐
Suicidal thoughts	☐
Drug and alcohol abuse	☐

Sources: HeretoHelp, BC Partners for Mental Health and Addictions Information, **http://www.heretohelp.bc.ca/visions/trauma-and-victimization-vol3/war-trauma-in-refugees**, *Caring for Kids New to Canada*, Canadian Paediatric Society, **http://www.kidsnewtocanada.ca/mental-health/ptsd**, eMentalHealth.ca , **http://m.ementalhealth.ca/index.php?m=article&ID=8885&r=Winnipeg-Regional-Health-Authority**, Sirin, Selcuk R. and Rogers-Sirin, Lauren, *The Educational and Mental Health Needs of Syrian Refugee Children*, Migration Policy Institute, October 2015

The Symptoms Checklist is not a diagnostic tool. It is to be used only as a guide to indicate when you may need to seek professional care. Remember that there is professional help available in Canada to treat mental health issues such as depression or PTSD. Ask for help.

If you or someone in your family is suicidal, call 911 or go to your closest Emergency Department at your local hospital

CHAPTER 3: SETTLEMENT AND INTEGRATION

Settlement

You have finally arrived in Canada. What do you need to do immediately, in the next few weeks and in the next year?

This section will answer your questions and provide information on adapting successfully and learning how to integrate into Canadian society.

Your First Week

Upon arrival in Canada, there are some things you need to attend to immediately. Buy a street map at a local convenience store to help you navigate. Start exploring. Walk around. Take different bus routes to see where you live.

> **You MUST apply for a Social Insurance Number (SIN) and a medical insurance health card**

Social Insurance Number (SIN)

A Social Insurance Number (SIN) is a nine-digit number that you require to work in Canada or to receive government benefits. A SIN is issued to one person only. You will need your SIN for your lifetime. Parents or legal guardians can apply for a SIN on behalf of a minor child. Children who are 12 years of age or older can apply for their own SINs. There is no fee for obtaining a SIN.

You must apply in person at a local Service Canada Centre with original proof of your identity documents. You can find your local Service Canada Centre at: **www.servicecanada.gc.ca** or telephone: **1-800-206-7218**.

You must provide one of the following documents: Record of Landing issued before June 28, 2002, Permanent Resident Card, Verification of Status issued by Citizenship and Immigration Canada.

In addition to your primary document, you will need to provide one of the following supporting documents when you apply, if required: Certificate of Marriage, Divorce Certificate, Legal Change-of-Name Certificate, Adoption Order, Request to Amend Record of Landing or a Confirmation of Permanent Residence document. If your application is approved, you will receive your SIN card that day.

Apply for Benefits

If you are a government-assisted refugee, you will receive financial support from the Canadian government for up to one year from your date of arrival in Canada or until you can support yourself. If you are a privately sponsored refugee, depending on which program you were sponsored under, your private sponsor will assist you financially for one year. This may or may not be in partnership with the government, which will cover your costs for six months and your private sponsor for the next six months. There are also financial assistance programs for government-assisted refugees and loans for resettled refugees.

If you are a parent, there are a number of federal benefits you may be eligible to receive. You can ask how to apply at the Service Canada Centre when you apply for your SIN.

These benefits include the following:

- Universal Child Care Benefit: A taxable, $100 monthly payment to families for each child under the age of 6
- Canada Child Tax Benefit: A tax-free, monthly payment to help families raise children under 18 years of age based on your income tax returns
- Child Disability Benefit: A tax-free benefit for families who care for a child under 18 with a severe or prolonged impairment

Some provinces also provide additional benefits. Check the provincial or territorial website for more information on tax benefits to families.

Health Insurance

All Canadian permanent residents can apply for and be covered by government health insurance. You need to apply for a health insurance card as soon as you arrive. The provincial or territorial governments issue health cards.

If you arrived as a refugee, the Canadian government's Interim Federal Health Program (IFHP) provides temporary health-care coverage to those who are not eligible for provincial or territorial health insurance. To apply contact:
http://www.cic.gc.ca/english/refugees/outside/arriving-healthcare/individuals/apply-how.asp

You will need your health insurance card to receive medical care from doctors and at medical clinics and hospitals.

British Columbia, Ontario and New Brunswick require permanent residents to wait a certain period (up to three months) before receiving government health insurance. All other provinces provide healthcare coverage immediately.

If you are planning on living in one of these provinces, it is important to buy private health care insurance to cover this waiting period before you arrive.

If you plan to travel outside Canada, you must buy private travel insurance from an insurance company.

Medical Emergencies

There are different types of medical emergencies. For something that is life threatening, call 911 for an ambulance. The ambulance will quickly transport the patient to the hospital. There is a charge for the ambulance service, which differs in each province. Most workplaces offer extended health benefits that cover ambulance fees.

For other emergencies such as a broken bone, you are expected to transport the patient to the Emergency Room at your nearest local hospital.

For non-emergencies such as a sinus infection or sore throat, you can either make an appointment with your family doctor or attend a Walk-In Clinic. Walk-In Clinics are typically open 7 days a week and have different doctors on call to take non-emergency patients.

Register Your Children in School

> **Upon arrival, you MUST register your school-age children in elementary, middle or high school**

Visit your nearest local school or school board to register your child. When you register your child, you will need to bring: Permanent Resident Card, Record of Landing or Confirmation of Permanent Residence, your child's birth certificate and your child's vaccination certificate if available. If you do not have your child's birth certificate or vaccination certificate, you must still register your children in school. You will need to show some identification with your current address in Canada.

If you have records from your child's previous schools that are translated into English or French, bring them with you to the school when registering your child.

The school may assess your child to determine what grade they should be placed in and whether they need additional support. Many schools have settlement workers who can speak your language and can assist in answering your questions.

Buying Food and Household Goods

Most communities have one or more large supermarkets that sell all kinds of food and groceries. Some of the larger grocery store names include: Costco, IGA, Loblaw's, Safeway, Sobeys, The Real Canadian Superstore, No Frills and Wal-Mart. There are also many different "ethnic" grocery stores in larger communities.

In most cities in Canada, you will be able to find food from your home country. Many items are sold in the large supermarkets and at local ethnic grocery stores.

In Canada, you do not bargain for a lower price. All prices are set and displayed for each item. You will pay a provincial sales tax (PST) and a 5% federal sales tax (GST) on many goods and services. New Brunswick, Nova Scotia, Newfoundland and Labrador, Ontario and Prince Edward Island have a harmonized their provincial sales tax with GST. This is called HST.

There are shopping malls, which have a variety of different stores selling household goods, clothing and personal items. There are also second-hand and consignment stores that sell used clothing, furniture and other household items.

People also sell things they no longer need. You can find items online at **www.kijiji.ca** or at yard or garage sales (held at people's private homes usually on Saturday mornings during the nicer weather). You can negotiate/bargain for second-hand items sold online or at yard sales. When you first arrive in Canada, second-hand shops, purchasing items online and buying a second-hand car are more cost effective than buying new.

In the summer months, you can find fresh vegetables and fruits at local farmer's markets.

Banking

If you have not already done so in your home country, go to your local bank or credit union to open a bank account. You will need to show your landed immigrant papers and any other identification you have to prove your residency.

Buy a Cell Phone (Mobile)

It is a smart idea to purchase a cell phone and mobile network plan shortly after you arrive. The three largest service providers in Canada are Rogers Wireless, Bell Mobility and TELUS. A cell phone will allow you to contact different service organizations.

Immigrant Settlement Services

Canada wants and needs immigrants. To help you get a good start, the Government of Canada funds immigrant/refugee-serving agencies in each province.

Immigrant-serving organizations assist newcomers settle, obtain language training, find work, get a mentor and integrate. There is no fee for these services. Most provide services to Permanent Residents for their first three years in Canada.

You can find your local settlement agency at:
http://www.cic.gc.ca/english/newcomers/map/services.asp

For agencies that specifically serve refugees:
http://ccrweb.ca/en/members#zoom=3&lat=52.26816&lon=-96.50391&layers=TB

Your First Few Weeks

Take a Tour of Where You Live

Many cities offer half or full-day sightseeing tours. A sightseeing tour will provide you with information about the city. It will give you a sense of what different parts of the city look like. You can ask questions about different locations.

> **Before you decide what neighbourhood you want to live in, it is a good idea to spend some time discovering the place where you have located.**

Another way to find out about different neighborhoods is to take different bus routes to explore what each is like. You can either stay on the bus or get off and walk around. For those of you who live in a town or rural area, walk around and see the sites.

If you have the time, volunteer for Meals on Wheels, a charitable organization that delivers midday meals to the elderly. You can be a driver or a food deliverer. You can commit to one route or be a spare and be called when no one else is available to go on different routes. It is a great way to learn about where you live, while at the same time meeting some different people.

Find Medical Care

Within a short time after your arrival, you will need to find a family doctor and dentist. How do you find a family doctor, dentist or optometrist? Most cities and provinces have a website or telephone number, which you can call to find the names of doctors in your area that are accepting new patients.

Make an appointment to see your new family doctor. You can do this by telephoning the doctor's receptionist. Take all your available medical records with you to the appointment.

To find a dentist or an optometrist in Canada, look in the telephone Yellow Pages or online. Ask your family or friends for names of dentists that they know. Then, call to see if the dentist is accepting new patients.

Dentists are not free in Canada. Different dentists charge different rates, usually based on how long they have been in practice. Many employers offer health benefits that cover a portion of dental charges.

Find a More Permanent Home

By now, you have checked out different neighborhoods and have narrowed down your search of where you want to live. You must decide if you rent or purchase. Most newcomers decide to rent and wait a few years until they purchase a home.

You need to determine a budget of what you can afford to pay monthly. Here are some of the costs to consider:
- Rent
- Tenant or Home Owner Insurance
- Utilities
    - Heat
    - Water
    - Electricity
    - Telephone
    - Internet service
    - Cable for television

Start going to see different rental apartments. Ask questions about what is included in the rent. Ask what types of people live in the apartment? Are there families or mainly seniors or single people? What schools are nearby? What bus, subway or light-rail train routes are nearby? Are there grocery stores nearby? What is the maximum number of people that can live in the apartment?

When you decide on a place to rent, here is a checklist for you to use.

Rental Checklist

Checklist	☑
Read, understood and signed written tenancy agreement	
Checked rental unit for damage and recorded/photographed	
Got landlord to sign the list of damages and kept copy	
Arranged for utilities not provided by landlord: electricity, water, heat, cable for television, telephone and internet service	
Bought tenants or home owner's insurance	

Buy a Computer or Laptop

Purchasing a computer or laptop and Internet access should be another priority as most jobs advertised in Canada accept applications on-line. You will be able to search for jobs, write your cover letters and resumes, and submit your applications if you have a computer with Internet access. Public libraries also have computers that you can use until you are able to afford your own computer.

If you do not know how to use a computer, there are usually local social service agencies that provide free or low cost computer lessons. Ask your counsellor at the local refugee-serving agency where you can take free computer lessons.

Credential Recognition for Regulated Professions

Before you arrived in Canada, you hopefully contacted your regulatory body in the province you planned to arrive in.

Each province regulates certain professions. If you worked in what is a regulated profession in Canada, you may be able to get re-certified to work in that profession in Canada.

Visit your profession's regulatory body to begin or continue the process of getting licensed in your profession or trade.

If you are asked to take a specific English course for your profession, attend more courses at college, university and/or your professional organization, participate in a Bridging Training Program or obtain clinical or workplace experience before you are allowed to write your licensing exam, consider the cost and time of participating.

Weigh the pros and cons. Can you afford to do this when you first arrive? Should you consider an alternative career or a new profession? If you can afford the time and money it costs, you should strongly pursue your licensure.

Your First Year

Find Childcare

According to the law, children under the age of 12 cannot be left at home alone in Canada. Once you are working, you will need daycare for your young children.

There are several different options for childcare in Canada: licensed daycares, nursery schools, home-based daycares and school based before-and-after school programs. Each will charge a daily fee to provide services. Many have long waiting lists, so you may consider putting your child on a wait list even when you are unemployed, as you may be employed by the time the child is accepted.

> **It is best to find a childcare before you start working and put your child's name on the waiting list**

Get a Driver's License

You need a driver's license to drive in Canada. It is illegal to drive without a license. Driver's licenses are issued by the province or territory where you live. In most provinces, you must be 16 years of age to legally drive. You must carry your driver's license with you at all times when you are driving. Both men and women drive in Canada.

If you have a valid driver's license from your country or an international driver's license, you may be able to drive for a short time period after you arrive. Contact your local provincial government driver-licensing department to enquire.

The process for getting a driver's licence varies across provinces and territories. You may have to write a written exam on the rules of the road and then take a driving test.

If you are an experienced driver, it is a good idea to pay a professional driving school for a couple of lessens to refresh you on the driving rules in Canada and parallel parking.

If you are a new driver, it is important to take driving lessons from a professional driving school. You can practice driving with a licensed driver who is a family member or friend before taking the road test.

Once you have your driver's license, it is valid for a period of time before you have to pay for its renewal.

Purchasing Car Insurance

There are different options for car insurance depending on the province where you live.

In some provinces, car insurance is available through private insurance companies. Ontario has the highest private auto insurance rates in Canada. Alberta is the second most costly. Driver's insurance rates are determined by actual risk factors. For example, a younger, inexperienced driver would pay a higher rate.

In provinces with private car insurance, it is important to get quotes from different insurers prior to making a decision about which one to buy.

> **It is strictly illegal to drive without car insurance in Canada**

Public car insurance, such as in Saskatchewan and Manitoba, coverage is provided by the provincial government. It can be purchased through any local insurance dealer. Standard rates apply to every driver, regardless of age or gender.

Traffic Laws

> **Driving laws are strictly enforced in Canada, and penalties for breaking the law are generally costly**

There are too many laws to list fully here so you will need to learn and understand traffic laws. The two most important to know are that you must have a driver's license to drive and you must be covered by car insurance to drive.

> **If the police stop you for breaking a traffic law, stay in your car. The police officer will come to your car to talk to you. You will be asked to provide your driver's license and automobile registration.**

Drinking And Driving

Most provinces have very strict laws about driving after you have been drinking alcohol. If the police stop you after you have been drinking alcohol, you could have your vehicle taken away, lose your driver's license, pay fines, and possibly go to jail.

Parking Tickets

If you park in a no parking area or if you do not put enough money in a parking meter, you may have to pay a fine. Be sure to check the signs on the street that will tell you, if and when, you can park on that street. You cannot park in front of a fire hydrant (which fire fighters use to get water to a fire), or at places where public buses stop to pick up passengers.

Seat Belts and Child Safety Seats

Seat belts are mandatory to wear for all passengers and drivers in every province in Canada. Fines for not wearing seatbelts can be costly.

Child car seat legislation is different in each province, so it is important to know and understand the law. If you have an infant, child or children that require car seats, buy approved age appropriate car seats that meet the Canada Motor Vehicle Safety Standards. Ask how to properly install the car seat into a vehicle.

Speeding

In most cities in Canada, the speed limit is 50 kilometres per hour (km/h) unless otherwise posted. Outside the city, the speed limit is higher usually between 90 – 110 km/hr. In some places, the speed limit is reduced to 30 km/hr near schools. Fines for driving faster than the speed limit can be very expensive.

Texting and Hands Free Talking

It is against the law to text or use a handheld device such as a cell phone (mobile) while driving.

Attending College or University

One way to improve your competiveness is to study in Canada. You can take a whole new career path or you can take a few courses that compliment your foreign education.

Many newcomers think that if they take more education, they will be more employable. This is not necessarily true. Educational qualifications are only assessed during the screening process for the job interview. Most employers are looking for more than just education. They want you to have the soft skills necessary to work in the Canadian workplace. Sometimes, volunteering, doing an internship or working in a related career will weigh more than a list of qualifications.

> **Canadian employers may not recognize your foreign education because they do not understand how it equates to Canadian education.**

You can improve your competiveness by taking a few courses that compliment your foreign education or you can take a whole new career path.

In Canada, there are different types of post-secondary education and institutions. You want to select an institution that is "recognized". "Recognized" means that the provincial or territorial government has granted the authority to that institution to grant degrees, diplomas, and certificates.

To be accepted into university or college you must meet the admission requirements. Each university and college determines its own admission requirements for each program. Each university and college assesses foreign education for admissions along with language skills. You must have the appropriate language level to qualify for the academic program.

College

Colleges offer degree, diploma and certificate programs that you pay tuition to attend. College programs are typically under 3 years in length. Many include a work co-op experience where you gain practical work experience, learn about the Canadian workplace culture and get work references. Generally speaking, College tuition is about half the cost of university tuition.

University

Universities offer degree programs that you pay tuition to attend. There are three levels of degrees: Bachelors, Master's and Doctorate. Undergraduate degree programs where you obtain a Bachelor's degree are typically 3-4 years in length.

> **Both university and college graduates are highly respected in Canada**

Settlement Checklist

	To Do	☑
1	Apply for Social Insurance Number	
2	Apply for Health Insurance Card	
3	Register Children in School	
4	Set up a Bank or Credit Union Account	
5	Apply for Government Benefits	
6	Buy a Cell Phone and Cell Phone Plan	
7	Visit local Immigrant-Serving Agency	
8	Take a Tour of Where You Live	
9	Find a Doctor and Dentist	
10	Find a more Permanent Home	
11	Buy a Computer or Laptop with Internet Access	
13	Find Childcare	
14	Get Driver's License and Car Insurance	
15	Improve English or French Language Skills	
16	Participate in community activities	
17	Get help if you need it	
18	Be patient and Do Not Give Up	

CHAPTER 4: FINDING A JOB

Preparing to Find a Job

You need to determine if your occupation is a regulated or non-regulated occupation in the province you are living in. If you are in a regulated profession or trade, you must obtain certification before you can practice your profession. Some professions are regulated in some provinces and not in others. If you are in a non-regulated profession, you can apply for jobs immediately.

The Government of Canada's Job Bank provides information about skill requirements and job opportunities based on your occupation and location: **www.jobbank.gc.ca**

Getting a License to Practice Your Profession

Each profession and trade has different certification requirements depending on the province. You cannot practice or work in your profession without a license if it is a regulated occupation.

Step 1: Determine if your profession is regulated in the province you reside in. Commonly regulated professions include ones where the public's safety is concerned including healthcare, financial and legal services, engineering and most skilled trades.

Step 2: Determine what regulatory organization is responsible for providing you with an assessment of your qualifications and certification.

Step 3: Contact the regulatory organization to see what procedures and documents are required to become licensed. If you do not have documents, ask the regulatory organization if they can still assess you. The Canadian Information Centre for International Credentials (**www.cicic.ca**) has information about licensing and regulatory bodies across Canada.

The licensing process typically has three components:
1. Assessment of your educational documents
2. Assessment of your work experience
3. Writing the licensing exam

Depending on the results of the assessments, you may be asked to upgrade or attend a Bridging Program or you may be eligible to write the exam directly.

Bridging Programs are designed to give internationally educated professionals training and experience to fill the gaps to prepare for licensing and working in a Canadian workplace. They are typically offered through joint programs between the regulatory body and a university or college.

Getting licensed can be costly and take a long time. While you are in the process of licensing, you should determine your transferable skills and consider alternative careers.

Transferable Skills

Transferable skills are employment skills that you can take with you from one job to another. For example, analytical, communication, computer, creativity, leadership, listening, numeracy, organizational, problem-solving, supervisory, teamwork and time management skills are all transferable skills. No matter what profession or trade you are in, these skills are important to all employers.

Transferable skills may also be referred to as the soft skills you bring to the workplace. Employers look for employees who can demonstrate suitable transferable skills. It is important for you to identify and be able to provide examples of your transferable skills.

How can you identify your transferable skills?

Start by analyzing each of the jobs you have held, to identify what skills you used doing those jobs. These are the transferable skills that will become part of your resume and can be used to answer job interview questions.
When looking for a job in Canada, you may not have direct experience working in a particular area, but you will be able to describe to a prospective employer how the skills you have acquired throughout your career are transferable to the new job.

During job interviews, hiring managers often ask more questions about your soft skills or your transferable skills than your technical skills. Interviewers expect you to provide concrete examples of your tranferable skills to show the employer that you are a "good fit" for the position.

Use the Transferable Skills Inventory to identify your transferable skills along with examples.

Transferable Skills Inventory

Transferable Skills	Able to:	☑	Examples:
Accept and Provide Constructive Criticism	Offer and receive valid and well-reasoned positive and negative opinions about the work of others in a friendly manner		
Analytical and Problem Solving	Assess a situation, gather relevant information and solve both complex and uncomplicated problems and concepts		
Communication	Express yourself clearly in both verbal and written form		

Transferable Skills	Able to:	☑	Examples:
Conflict Resolution	Reach a mutually acceptable agreement when there is a disagreement or dispute		
Continuous Learning	Continue to always develop and improve your knowledge and skills		
Creativity	Solve problems through new and innovative methods		
Flexible	Adapt to change without resistance		

Transferable Skills	Able to:	☑	Examples:
Human Relations	Use interpersonal skills for resolving conflict, relating to and helping people		
Initiative	Readiness and ability to take action and follow through with a plan, project or task		
Intercultural	Demonstrate understanding of other cultures and skills to interact in a cross-culturally sensitive manner		

Transferable Skills	Able to:	☑	Examples:
Internet and Social Media	Understand how to use computer, word processing, internet, email, spreadsheets, presentation software		
Interpersonal	Communicate effectively with colleagues, clients and various stakeholders		
Leadership	Influence and inspire others in support of a common goal		
Listening	Listen attentively and clearly articulate the purpose and content of a conversation		

Transferable Skills	Able to:	☑	Examples:
Local Language Skills	Communicate verbally and in written form using local jargon and idioms used in your area and in your particular industry		
Management	Supervise, direct and guide staff in the successful completion of tasks and goals		
Organization	Use your time, energy and resources in an effective manner		
Planning	Conceptualize future needs and solutions for meeting those needs		

Transferable Skills	Able to:	☑	Examples:
Presentation Skills	Present in a confident and clear manner to small and large groups		
Small Talk	Chat about common and local topics such as weather, sports, restaurants, movies		
Teamwork	Collaborate with others to achieve a desired result		
Time Management	Set priorities and meet deadlines		

Alternative Career

Becoming licensed in your profession in Canada can be a long, costly and challenging process. Many internationally educated professionals need to complete some form of skills upgrading or education before they can write their licensing exam.

As a result, you might consider pursuing an alternative career where you can transfer your current skills, knowledge, education, and work experience to another profession. Some individuals choose an alternative career as a permanent choice. Others choose a related career while pursuing licensing of their profession. The decision is up to you.

Following are some examples of professions and alternative or related careers.

Profession	Alternative Career
Construction Worker	• Cabinetmaker • Grounds Maintenance • Woodworker
Engineer	• Supply Chain Management • Technician or Technologist • Technical Consultant or Sales
Medical Laboratory Technologist	• Health Information Technologist • Pathologist Assistant • Technical Sales Specialist
Nurse	• Healthcare Aide • Healthcare Educator • Medical Sales Representative

Profession	Alternative Career
Teacher	• Corporate Trainer • Academic Advisor • Sales Representative
Social Worker	• Community Worker • Counsellor • Settlement Worker

Finding a Job

Like most newcomers to Canada, you will face many barriers in finding employment at your skill level. Once employed, you will also face many implicit and overt barriers.

As with many newcomers, you will also feel pressure to find a job as soon as possible to fulfill financial commitments and to feel like you have re-established yourself professionally in Canada.

> **Take advantage of all the settlement services and programs provided where you live.**
>
> **If you do not have adequate English or French language skills, attend language classes.**

> **To thrive in the Canadian workplace, one must be fluent in the language of their province and in the language of their profession. So take the opportunity and time to acquire appropriate language skills.**

When you begin your job search, you will need a Canadian-style cover letter and resume. You must also be prepared for a Canadian-style interview.

Do research to find companies and organizations that hire people in your field. Visit job search websites such as:
- **http://www.jobbank.gc.ca/home-eng.do?lang=eng**
- **www.indeed.ca**
- **www.wowjobs.ca**
- **www.workopolis.com**

There are several things you may need to have before you can obtain a good job in your field:

- Communication skills at the appropriate level to work successfully in your profession
- Accreditation of your profession, if regulated
- A professional network
- Soft skills and possibly Canadian work experience
- Skills to write a Canadian-style resume and cover letter

- Skills on how to answer Canadian-style interview questions
- Knowledge and understanding of Canadian workplace culture

Workplace Communication Skills

Communication skills are one of the most important skills you need to settle successfully in Canada and find a good job. In Canada, you are eligible for free language classes.

Many newcomers, who speak some English or French, make the mistake of thinking that their language skills are adequate, and they immediately start looking for employment.

They choose not to attend language classes. You need to have the appropriate language level plus understanding of local communication to be successful. You may find yourself being unemployed or underemployed if you do not have the language skills employers demand.

Communication is more than just speaking a language. It is being able to express yourself effectively in a manner that is appropriate to the location where you are living. What this means is that you have to be familiar with the local jargon, colloquial expressions, non-verbal behaviours and humour.

| **Do not overestimate your language skills** |

> **Employers have much higher expectations than immigration officials and demand higher-level communication skills**

The common measurement tool used in Canada for English language assessment is the Canadian Language Benchmark (CLB) test. For French, the language assessment it is Niveaux de compétence linguistique canadiens (NCLC). Language assessments are free of charge. Your local refugee-serving agency can refer you for the language assessment test.

To get a good job, generally speaking, you need to score a minimum of CLB or NCLC 7 for speaking, reading, listening and writing. Some professions require a higher language level based on the demands of their occupation. For example, nurses need a higher language level.

If you are below the minimum score in any category, you should strongly consider taking a language class.

Common Canadian Terms and Idioms

Every country and language has its own jargon and colloquial expressions. Unless you understand the terms and idioms used in Canada and in your profession, you will not be proficient and effective in your profession.

> **Idioms are phrases, which people use in everyday language, which do not make sense, but are understood.**

Your profession may also use acronyms and technical terms that may be unfamiliar to you. It is important to learn and understand these terms for you to be successful in your career.

> **When you hear an expression, idiom or phrase that you do not understand, ask what the other speaker is trying to say.**

A list of some common Canadian terms and idioms can be found in Appendix 1.

Networking

> **In Canada, 80% of all jobs are never advertised. This is called the "hidden" job market.**

As a new immigrant, you may only know a few people in Canada. You will have to actively work to build and develop your personal and professional network.

Networking is about building connections and long-term relationships with professional contacts. Networking is an effective strategy to help uncover hidden job opportunities.

The benefits of networking for you are:

- Build relationships
- Increase opportunities
- Raise profile
- Gain advice and support

- Generate referrals
- Make new friends

Learning how to network effectively is one of the most powerful tools an individual can use to advance their personal and professional life.

Here are some steps for to become a successful networker.

How to Become a Successful Networker

Steps		What to Do	☑
Prepare Ahead:			
1	**Identify Your Strengths**	• Develop a list of your talents, strengths and skills sets	
2	**Identify People**	• Identify people you already know • Identify where you can meet new people, i.e., ethnic associations, language classes, community centres, gyms, volunteer placements, mentorship placements, informational meetings, LinkedIn, Twitter • Identify professional network opportunities, i.e., conferences, professional association meetings	
3	**Research**	• Research the company, industry or career of your contacts.	

4	**Plan what you want to say**	• Identify how you can help people now and in the future • Develop some questions to ask about your contact's areas of expertise • Prepare a 1-2 minute introductory script highlighting your name, background, skills and accomplishments (often referred to as an Elevator Pitch) • Avoid asking for a job
•	**Attend Networking Event**	
5	**Dedicate Time for Networking**	• Set goals for yourself of how many networking contacts you will connect with each week • Identify attendees and who you would like to talk with
6	**Be Visible**	• Focus on meeting new people • Engage people in conversation • Ask for information and advice, not a job • Try to find common interests • Ask for introductions and referrals
7	**How to Finish**	• Towards the end of any conversation, ask how you can be of help • Exchange business cards (make one for yourself if you are not employed) • Thank them for the conversation and tell them you are looking forward to keeping in contact

Follow-Up and Follow Through		
8	**Stay Connected**	• Keep in touch with your new contacts • Send a thank you email or card to your new contact for any help, referrals or resources s/he shared
9	**Stay Active**	• Stay active on social media with your contacts and prospective contacts • If you made a commitment to help, follow through with your promise

Elevator Pitch

An elevator pitch is a very brief summary about you and your value to a prospective employer. The name "elevator pitch" reflects the idea that it is possible to deliver a summary about you in the time it takes to ride an elevator – approximately 30 seconds.

You should be prepared to attract interest, capture your audience's attention quickly, and highlight what makes you unique. You use your elevator pitch when networking and in job interviews.

Here are the steps to developing your elevator pitch:
- Greeting and Introduction (shake hands): Name and profession
- Emphasize concrete accomplishments and skills
- Highlight your uniqueness: Think about what really sets your work and experience apart from others in your industry.
- Select accomplishments and skills that would be of the most interest to your listener
- State what you can do for them

Be prepared to answer questions. Let the listener hear the commitment in your voice and your words. Make direct eye contact.

Keep it short. Refine your elevator pitch as your professional life continues to grow and change.

Canadian Work Experience

Many Canadian employers are unsure whether you will be a "good fit" in their organization. A "good fit" means you have the required skills, experience, work ethic and personality of those currently working in the organization.

The employer may wonder if you have sufficient language skills and are aware of Canadian workplace standards, technologies and culture. Employers may eliminate you from the selection and hiring process because of their concerns. Note that it is illegal in the Province of Ontario to require Canadian work experience.

There are several ways to gain Canadian work experience:
- Volunteer
- Job shadow
- Internship
- Temporary work

Volunteering

Volunteering is where you work for no salary. It is very common and highly valued in Canada. Most Canadians volunteer throughout their lifetime and career.

For you as a newcomer to Canada, volunteering offers many benefits:

- You will significantly improve your communication skills and knowledge of soft skills
- You will learn business etiquette
- Make new friends
- Build your network
- Gain practical work experience and Canadian job references.

You can find volunteer opportunities at:
http://volunteer.ca/volunteer-centres

Job Shadowing

Job Shadowing is where you ask people in your professional network if you can spend some time in their company learning about the different jobs related to your field. You follow someone around for a day. You will learn about the workplace culture, business communications and small talk, and may gain Canadian job references.

Internships

Internships are where you work for an employer and the government subsidizes your salary. Internships are not offered for all professions. You can enroll in internships through your local settlement agency. There may be wait lists so put your name in advance on the wait list.

Mentorship

A mentor is someone who guides others to help them achieve their personal and/or career goals. The role can be informal or formal. They can be a counselor, a trusted resource, a coach, a role model, a senior manager or someone who provides emotional support.

Typically, mentors share knowledge, provide guidance and advice on careers, resources, workplace culture and networking opportunities, and offer encouragement to the mentee. Mentors help you feel comfortable with self-promotion, a Canadian tactic for getting noticed and getting a job.

> **A mentor can play a strong role in easing your transition into the Canadian workplace**

When you are employed, ask your manager if the organization has a mentor program or if someone could be your mentor. Ask that mentor to help you understand how to interpret the Canadian workplace culture, the organizational culture and what the expectations of being a "good employee" in that company entail.

Ask the mentor to help you understand the rules and customs of your new environment - what are the expectations of teamwork, expectations of managers, constructive feedback, how to engage in small talk, concepts of time and punctuality, how to resolve workplace conflict, workplace etiquette and what equality in the workplace actually means.

Writing Cover Letters

A cover letter is your sales pitch to the employer telling them why they should contact you for an interview and why you are the best fit for the job. Your cover letter is your first opportunity to impress an employer. It should compel the employer to want to read your resume.

Cover letters identify the job you are applying for and provide additional information about your skills and experiences that are not highlighted in your resume.

> **Your cover letter must capture the attention of the Hiring Manager**

When writing your cover letter, the first step is to analyze the job advertisement and determine the most important skills the employer is looking for. The next step is to address how you will meet the employer's needs.

The first sentence of your cover letter should emphasize the major selling points and skills that you would bring to the job.

The body of the letter is used to demonstrate that you can perform the duties listed in the job advertisement. Think about what you have accomplished in your past jobs and which are transferable skills, experience and attributes to the new job. Emphasize this in the body of the letter and include results in your cover letter.

Conclude your cover letter with a powerful statement about discussing your skills, experience and achievements in more detail at an interview.

Your cover letter must be easy to read. Use Arial 11 pt. font or Time New Roman 12 pt. font with normal margins. A cover letter is 1-2 pages maximum in length. It should contain no spelling or grammatical errors.

Most settlement agencies will help you prepare a basic cover letter or you can hire someone to write your cover letter for you.

Sample cover letters can be found in Appendix 2.

Resume (CV) Writing

When you are applying for jobs in Canada, you will be expected to submit a resume with your cover letter. Your resume has to be Canadian-style and customized to the job you are applying for.

What is a Canadian-style resume?

It is a summary of your work experience and education highlighting your major accomplishments. It is maximum 2 pages in length and is written in Arial 11 pt. font or Times New Roman 12 pt. font with normal margin sizes. It does not contain a photo or personal information such as gender, age, marital status, father's name or religion. It does not contain school grades. It uses action verbs to describe each talent, strength and accomplishment. Action verbs can be found on the Internet.

Most settlement agencies will help you prepare a basic resume listing your different employers and responsibilities. However, you should be aware that the resume will not be customized to each job advertisement and it is unlikely to describe your accomplishments. You will be expected to do this on your own.

Remember that you will be competing with Canadian-born applicants who know how to write a customized cover letter and resume. You want your resume to be noticed amongst the hundreds of applications that employers receive for each job advertised.

The most important thing to remember when writing a resume is to customize it to the job advertisement. Ensure that you address all *must have* and *desired* requirements. Include your accomplishments not your job responsibilities. Make sure you quantify your accomplishments. Make sure there are no errors in spelling or grammar.

> **Resumes need to be quantified and show accomplishments rather than a list of duties and responsibilities**

Sample resumes can be found in Appendix 3.

Job Interview Preparation

You must be able to describe your skills, experience and accomplishments in a way Canadian employers can understand.

Canadian employers want their employees to possess skills specific to the job, the occupation and the employer. Employers want you to have transferable soft skills.

> **You may find that the interview questions relate more to your soft skills than your education, occupational skills or work experience**

When you are contacted for an interview, do your research about the company. Read all documents you can about the company's mission, goals, policies, program and services. Visit the organization before your interview. Walk around the public spaces of the organization to get a sense of how employees dress and interact.

During your interview, you may be asked: *What do you know about this company or why do you want to work here?* The employer is testing you to see if you prepared for the interview by conducting research. It shows that you took initiative and possess research skills.

Canadian employers typically use behavioural interview questions. Behavioural interview questions are used to get an idea if you have the skills and competencies required for the job. They focus more on experiences, behaviours, knowledge, skills and abilities. The best way to prepare for behavioural interview questions is to analyze the job advertisement for skills and attributes the employer is wanting. These are the skills that the interviewers will most likely focus on.

Think about potential interview questions and responses. Your responses must be concise and to the point supported by real-life examples.

You may be asked questions about your teamwork skills to determine if you work well with others. If staff will be reporting to you, then expect questions about how you lead, manage and motivate others. You may be asked about how you handled conflict or solved problems or situations.

You may be asked about your strengths and your weaknesses. If you are asked to describe a weakness, state it in a positive way. For example: *I am such a dedicated worker that sometimes I spend too much time on work and not enough time with my family. I have to learn to be more balanced.*

Do research to find examples of behavioural questions you might be asked in your profession.

You will also be asked if you have any questions at the end of the interview, so prepare questions to ask. Do not ask questions about the salary and benefits as these are things you negotiate once you are offered the position.

If you get nervous during interviews, here are two strategies:

- Take a deep breath before you respond to a question
- Ask the interviewer to repeat the question as a tactic to give you more time to think of a response

You are allowed to take documents and notes into an interview. The notes can be reminders of how you plan to answer potential questions. Many settlement agencies offer interview preparation courses that you can attend free of charge.

You want to make a good first impression. Plan what you will wear to the interview. Depending on the occupation, you should dress slightly more formal than what people normally wear to work.

Men should wear socks and shoes. Avoid sandals. There is an old rule that says women should only wear white shoes and carry a white handbag from May 24 - September 24. This rule is not strictly enforced, but for a job interview, you might want to take it under consideration.

Avoid wearing perfume or strong smelling aftershave. Many Canadian workplaces are scent-free.

The best way to answer behavioural interview questions is to use the STAR technique:

Situation:	Present a recent situation or challenge you found yourself in.
Task:	Describe what you had to achieve.
Action:	Describe what you did, why you did it and what the alternatives were.
Results:	Present the outcomes of your actions, how you met your objectives, and what you learned from the experience.

Sample interview questions and answers can be found in Appendix 4.

Job Offer

You are offered a job. Now, it is the time to decide if you accept the job offer. You start by negotiating the salary. Ask what benefits are included. Ask about hours and days of work, policy on overtime, pension plans, and vacations. Ask if you are unionized (union fees will be deducted from your salary). Then, decide if you accept or reject the offer.

If you do not get a job offer after the interview, call or email the HR person or interviewer and ask what you can do to improve your interview skills and other skill areas you need to develop. Thank the person for their feedback and for the opportunity to be interviewed.

Deductions from Your Paycheque

Pensions

The Canada Pension Plan (CPP) is a program for workers and their families. CPP provides pensions and benefits when contributors retire, become disabled or die. Most individuals who work in Canada contribute to CPP. Your employer will deduct CPP contributions directly from your paycheque. The amount you pay is based on your salary.

Your employer may also have a pension plan that you contribute to each pay period. Deductions will be taken off your paycheque for the company's pension plan.

Taxes

All residents of Canada pay income tax on income they have received throughout the year. Your employer will deduct income taxes directly from your paycheque. The amount of income tax deducted will be based on your salary and family circumstances, i.e., single versus married.

When you file your Income Tax return by April 30th of each year, the government will determine if you paid too much, if so, you will get a refund. If you did not pay enough, then you will be asked to pay more. You can obtain income tax forms at any post office or online.

If you leave Canada for an extended period of time, notify the Canadian Revenue Agency, as you may need to file an income tax return for that year.

For more information about taxes, you can ask your employer. You can contact the Canada Revenue Agency by phone or online at: **www.cra-arc.gc.ca**

You can also register online for a CRA account, which will give you access to your tax information and your Canadian Pension Plan.

Other Deductions

The employer will also deduct from your paycheque: medical and dental premiums, life insurance premiums, long-term disability premiums, and employment insurance premiums.

Employees' Rights

Knowing your employment and human rights is important once you gain employment.

Employment Standards

In Canada, there are provincial and federal labour laws to protect employees and employers. These laws set minimum wages, hours of work and overtime pay, health and safety standards, parental leave, annual paid vacation, severance pay, meal and coffee breaks, and protection for children. These are described in the Employment Standards for each province and territory and in federal labour standards for those that fall under the federally regulated businesses or industries.

To find out more information online, see the following resources:
Provincial Workplace Standards:
www.esdc.gc.ca/en/jobs/workplace/index.page

Federal Labour Laws: **www.labour.gc.ca/eng/home.shtml**

> You have the right to speak up in the workplace when your rights are being violated.
>
> Employers cannot refuse to pay you overtime.
>
> Employers cannot force you to work excessive hours.
>
> Employers cannot fire you or have you deported if you refuse or complain about working overtime or other employee rights that are violated.

Workplace, Health and Safety

All workers in Canada have the right to work in a safe and healthy workplace. Each province and territory as well as the federal government, has its own legislation.

> You have the right to refuse unsafe work

If you become sick or are injured on the job, all provinces and territories provide worker's compensation. You must notify your employer immediately. Contact a physician and file a Worker's Compensation claim with your local workers compensation board.

Human Rights

Canada and each of its provinces and territories have human rights laws that prevent employers from discriminating against employees based on gender, age, ethnicity, race, religion, disability or sexual orientation.

If you are facing discrimination or harassment in the workplace, the first step is to try to resolve the issue with your employer. You also have the right to file a complaint with your local human rights agency.

> **Your employer cannot discipline you or penalize you for filing a human rights complaint**

For more information on human rights in your area, see:
www.cashra.ca/links.html

Finding a Job Checklist

	To Do	☑
1	Contact Regulatory Body if Profession is Regulated	
2	Identify Your Transferable Skills	
3	Start Building Your Network	
4	Volunteer	
5	Write Cover Letter	
6	Write Resume	
7	Apply for Jobs	
8	Prepare for Job Interviews	
9	Get help if you need it	
10	Be patient and Do Not Give Up	

CHAPTER 5: CULTURAL DIFFERENCES

Canada is a multicultural country with over 200 different languages spoken. Each province also has its own unique culture and sense of identity.

At work and where you live, you will need to have intercultural skills to be successful.

Try the Cultural Quiz to test your intercultural skills.

Cultural Quiz

1. Canadians believe it is acceptable to be a little late for a meeting.

    True   False

2. Business in Canada is more about building relationships as opposed to getting straight down to business.

    True   False

3. Canadians believe that women should take care of family and children.

    True   False

4. French Canadian friends may greet each other by lightly kissing on the cheeks.

    True   False

5. Canadians believe that maintaining eye contact with the person they are speaking with is respectful.

   True   False

6. Canadian managers are expected to manage in an authoritarian manner and employees are expected to unquestioningly follow the manager's suggestions and directions.

   True   False

7. Canadian men may offer their hand to a woman without waiting for her to extend hers first.

   True   False

8. People in Canada expect the right to be heard and listened to in meeting situations regardless of rank or status.

   True   False

9. In Canada, the boss is not expected to perform menial tasks such as making coffee for everybody or moving chairs in a meeting room.

   True   False

10. Gift giving is a tradition in the Canadian workplace.

    True   False

Answers to Cultural Quiz can be found on the next page.

Cultural Quiz Answers

1. false
2. false
3. false
4. true
5. true
6. false
7. true
8. true
9. false
10. false

Are you surprised at the answers?

Culture consists of many components:
- Values
- Interpretations of our perceptions
- Importance placed on time and space
- Childrearing practices
- Gestures
- Social etiquette
- How we grieve
- Systems: political, health, legal, education, social, etc.
- Behaviours
- Dress
- Food and eating habits
- Music and entertainment
- Celebrations

There will always be individual differences but for those who are of the same cultural background, there will be more shared values, behaviours and expectations.

Perceptions and Assumptions

Cultural differences are often misinterpreted. We may be looking at the same thing, but our interpretation of what we see may be very different.

For example, in many Middle Eastern cultures, it is rude and insulting to show the sole of the feet. In Canada, this body language has no meaning.

What happens when two people from these cultures interact and one person shows the sole of his or her feet? One will think nothing of this and the other person might feel he or she is being disrespected.

These two different perceptions and assumptions can affect how people interact in the workplace.

> **As a newcomer to Canada, it is important to learn to check your assumptions about Canadians and about the Canadian workplace**

Cultural Values and Beliefs

Review some generalized cultural differences between Canada and Some Other Parts of the World. Ask yourself: *What are your cultural beliefs and how to you display them through your behavior?*

Canada	Some Other Parts of the World
Individualist and Independent	Collectivist and Dependent on Group
Equality: Teamwork	Hierarchical: boss is authority
Task Oriented: Business 1st	Relationship Oriented: Friendship 1st
Structured Time: Be punctual and meet deadlines	Flexible Time
Direct Communication Style	Diplomatic Communication Style
Written-word Culture	Spoken-word Culture
Personal Privacy Valued	Concept of Personal Space Smaller
Gender equity	Gender division
Multicultural	Diverse

Where does your culture place on the chart?

For example, is your culture more collectivist? Is there a long-term commitment to the family and extended relationships? Is loyalty paramount? Do hiring and promotion decisions take into account family links? Do employees expect to be told what to do by their superiors?

If you come from a culture that is considered to be a hierarchical society where subordinates expect to be told what to do by managers, how will you deal with a Canadian workplace that is places value on equality?

Will you be able to speak up and give your opinion in meetings if your boss is present? Will you be able to call the CEO by his or her first name? Will you be able to change your management style?

In Canada, individual employees and teams are expected to share their expertise with the manager. The manager expects the individual employees to do their jobs and report if there is a problem that the manager needs to know about. Otherwise, the employee is expected to show initiative and do their jobs with little direction or interference from their superiors.

This is just one of many cultural differences that may create workplace challenges for you and for your Canadian employer.

If you come from a culture where time is flexible and things begin when people arrive, how will you adapt to a culture that values punctuality? If you come from a culture where women and men socialize separately, how will you handle having a female manager? These are just a few questions to consider.

When you come across behaviour that is unfamiliar or strange to you, ask for clarification. Do not assume and form your perceptions based on what could be a cultural misinterpretation.

Common Cultural Differences and Business Practices

Canadian workplaces are diverse with people of different ages, genders, levels of education, and ethnic and cultural backgrounds.

People see the world through their cultural filters. People from two different cultures can view the same behaviour differently. This makes working with different cultures challenging.

There are expected business norms in Canada and each organization will have its own workplace culture. In order for you to be successful and retain your job, you need to be aware of cultural differences and common business practices.

> **As a newcomer, you most likely will not have sufficient knowledge of Canadian culture, the Canadian workplace culture, the employer's organizational culture and the Canadian-equivalent professional culture of your profession or trade.**
>
> **These are huge barriers for gaining entry into a job, retaining that job and being promoted to higher-level positions.**

Greetings

In Canada, greetings do not hold as much social significance as they do in some other cultures.

When meeting a Canadian in the workplace, use a firm handshake accompanied by direct eye contact and a sincere smile when meeting and leaving your business associates. Typically a handshake is no more than three shakes or 2-3 seconds before releasing. Be prepared for men to hold their hand out to shake a woman's hand as she is considered his equal.

In Quebec only, for both sexes, people kiss once on each cheek when they greet one another. This is not common for non-French Canadian. Colleagues sometimes hug if they know each other well and have not seen each other for a long time.

Unlike some cultures, Canadians do not place their right hand on their heart when meeting someone as a way of expressing affection. Canadians do not prostrate or curtsy when meeting an elder or someone in a position of authority.

For initial introductions, use the appropriate professional title such as "Dr." or "Ms.", or "Mr." followed by the last name. Most likely you will quickly be invited to use first names.

> **Do not refer to Canadians as Auntie or Uncle, Mama or Ma'am or job title such as Engineer Smith**

When Canadians greet, they commonly say, "Hi. How are you?" They are not expecting you to reply with how you actually feel. This expression is simply a greeting. The common response is, "Good" or "Not Bad".

Greetings are not lengthy and usually do not include questions about health unless someone has been ill. Then, one might ask if they are feeling better.

The custom in Canadian workplaces is to greet people in the hallway and when you arrive or leave work with *hello, good morning* or *good night*.

Eye Contact

Staring or making limited eye contact is considered rude in Canada. You are expected to make eye contact when you are speaking with someone, including someone who is your superior such as a boss.

Typically, Canadians look at the person for three seconds, quickly and briefly look away, and then repeat.

Lack of eye contact in Canada is interpreted in many different ways. You may be considered shy, nervous or embarrassed. You may be considered a liar and dishonest or someone that has something to hide. Individuals may think you lack confidence or are distracted. These are just some of the assumptions people might make about you, if you do not make, the expected eye contact in Canada.

If you are uncomfortable making eye contact, practice with your family members or friends.

Punctuality

Generally, business meetings in Canada are well structured and time efficient. Punctuality for meetings, appointments and social events is a highly valued part of Canadian business culture.

If you are delayed more than a couple of minutes, you must inform your supervisor and/or colleagues of the delay and tell them exactly when you will arrive. Then, you must arrive at the said time or inform your colleagues if you are still delayed. If you arrive late, you are expected to quietly and quickly apologize.

Being late is considered rude and disrespectful. You will be viewed very badly if you are not punctual. In some French-speaking areas, the concept of time is a little more relaxed, but you will still be expected to arrive promptly.

Deadlines are very important and expected to be met as scheduled in Canada. Complete your work on time. If there is a problem, you are expected to inform your supervisor or team lead before the deadline and ask for suggestions, help or an extension. Do not wait until the deadline to apologize after the fact. It will not be looked at kindly.

Informality

As already noted, Canadians value equality. Business relationships are not viewed by order of rank, status, position or gender. As a result, interactions between a manager and a subordinate are largely informal.

Managers delegate and share power. In meetings, Canadians will expect everyone to participate and contribute to discussions from junior through to senior colleagues. They will not wait for their superior to tell them what to do. Employees are expected to take initiative, be self-directed and work with minimal guidance from above.

Managers and subordinates socialize together. Woman and men are treated equally. Age is irrelevant. Employees, supervisors, managers, directors and CEOs call each other by their first names.

Privacy and Personal Space

People's privacy and personal space is respected in Canada. Do not ask personal questions about someone's salary or family or personal health. Do not make what is perceived to be a negative comment about someone's appearance or weight. Do not borrow or take an item from someone's office or desk unless you ask beforehand.

Gossiping about others is considered to be very disrespectful.

Personal space comfort level varies across cultures. About 0.6096 meters or 2 feet (about arms-length) is acceptable for business interactions in Canada. In French-speaking areas, the personal space is generally reduced.

Leave Telephone Voice Messages

In Canada, employees schedule their time and are not always available to take your phone calls. You are expected to leave a voice message.

Do not hang up and call several times till you reach the individual. Employers and colleagues find this annoying and rude.

Do not arrive, in person, if whatever you need to communicate can be handled over the telephone or electronically.

Constructive Criticism

"Constructive criticism is the process of offering valid and well-reasoned opinions about the work of others, usually involving both positive and negative comments, in a friendly manner rather than an oppositional one. The purpose of constructive criticism is to improve the outcome."[48]

In Canada, constructive criticism is considered to be part of the growth and professional development of employees. It is delivered in a calm manner with the expectation that the person receiving the criticism will respond in a professional manner.

These are the five steps to giving constructive criticism:
1. Start with something positive.
2. Be constructive, specific, helpful and sensitive.
3. Refer to the person's behaviour or the specific situation, not the person.
4. Invite a collaborative discussion of the consequences.
5. Focus on behaviours that the other person can change.

This is how you should receive constructive criticism from others:
- Recognize the value of the feedback.
- Do not become defensive or be offended.
- Respect, accept and consider.
- Resolve any misunderstandings.
- Thank the other person for the feedback.
- Use the constructive criticism to improve.

---

[48] https://en.wikipedia.org/wiki/Constructive_criticism

Socializing

As Canadians tend to be more task-oriented, do not expect lengthy small talk during business. Small talk is however expected during breaks, while walking to a meeting or waiting for others to arrive, and sometimes when you first arrive or as you are leaving for the day.

In many Canadian workplaces, there is a strong division between home and work life. Talk about family is limited. Small talk is usually about the weather, traffic and sports.

> **If you do not know what co-workers are talking about, fake it by asking questions about their topic:** *Where is that restaurant? What kind of food do they serve? What hockey teams were playing? What was the final score?*
>
> **The other speakers will be unaware that you do not know what to say. They will appreciate your participation.**

Showing Initiative

Canadian employers expect you to be a self-starter and express your opinions and ideas. Someone who shows initiative is considered to be proactive, persistent and flexible.

Showing initiative means taking action in the workplace without being told what to do. Showing initiative is important in the Canadian workplace as it demonstrates your value at work and your capacity to develop as a leader.

Here are some tips for showing initiative:

- Be on alert for ideas for improvement
- Make suggestions for improvements
- Volunteer for projects and work teams
- Be prepared and decisive
- Help colleagues who need help

Relationships at Work

In Canada, relationships at work are for business-purposes. You are expected to get down to business rather than build relationships.

People are friendly but are not usually your friends. Although you may share life stories and experiences, socialize at work events and help each other, at the end of the day these are your colleagues. Only a small number may end up being your friends outside of work.

Trust is built by following through with what you say.

Expectations of Honesty

Canadian employers value honesty. You are expected to tell your supervisor when you do not understand, are uncertain about directions, cannot do the task or cannot meet the deadline.

"Yes" in Canada means you understand and will act. If you come from a culture where communication is more indirect, you may find it difficult to say "No" to a manager or superior.

> **Canadians expect you to say "no" if you cannot accomplish a task or meet deadlines.**
>
> **They expect you to tell them why it is impossible to accomplish the task or meet the deadline. You are not expected to tell the boss what you think s/he wants to hear.**
>
> **You are expected to be honest.**

Replying with a comment such as, "I will do my best" is considered to be a "Yes" I will do the task and meet the deadline.

The expression, *honesty is the best policy*, is highly valued in Canada. It means you are expected to tell the truth, even when it seems it would be useful to lie or apologize later.

Touching

Canadians generally do not touch one another or hold hands in the workplace. The only conventional touch is a handshake. You need to be mindful of, and sensitive to, others' tolerance for touch.

In Canada, it is acceptable for men and women to hold hands or link arms. This typically occurs in a romantic relationship.

In Canada, men do not commonly hold hands or link arms with other men nor do women commonly hold hands or link arms with other women as a sign of friendship. In Canada, same-sex couples hold hands or link arms. You may also observe women dancing together at social events in rural areas and small towns in Canada. This has nothing to do with their sexuality.

Names

In some cultures, a person's name reveals family relations. Canadian names are determined simply by the names the parents like when a child is born.

In Canada the given name is the first name. The second name may be a favourite name of the parents, a family name or the last name of the mother or father. The last name is usually the father's last name but in some cases it is the mother's last name or a hyphenated name consisting of both the mother and father's last name.

Food and Invitations

Eating is an important social activity in Canada. People often invite others for dinner or go out to a restaurant to share a meal. What may be different from your cultural practices is how Canadians deal with invitations and who pays for the meal.

It is considered polite in Canada to accept the invitation the first time, if one is able to attend. The process of declining the first invitation as a form of politeness does not exist in Canada.

Canadians do not commonly offer others some of what they are eating unless it is something exceptional that they want the other person to experience.

When dining out with friends, it is very common in Canada that the bill for the food will be split for each individual and/or couple. Rarely does the eldest or wealthiest pay for the whole meal. Men do not pay for women's meals unless they are on a romantic date. Friends and colleagues sometimes take turns paying the restaurant bill.

Politeness

Canadians are known for being extremely polite. Words such as, *Please*, *Thank You*, *You're Welcome* and *Sorry* are used often. For example, if a Canadian accidentally bumps into someone, both individuals will briefly apologize.

Canadians consider it polite to wait their turn. This applies to all pubic interaction. People will stand in line at cafeteria's, in banks, at grocery stores and at entertainment events. It is extremely rude to push through people. People are served on a first come, first serve basis. Status, age and gender do not affect who gets served first in Canada.

Speaking Your First Language at Work

Speaking your first language with colleagues from your home country sometimes creates an uncomfortable work environment for non-speakers.

You do have the right to speak in your own language when not dealing directly with clients or customers. However, be aware that some of your colleagues may feel left out or think you are ridiculing them if you only associate with co-workers from your own culture.

You need to be able to decipher on-the-job speaking and conversing on breaks. What you do on your meal and coffee breaks is your business. However, if you have colleagues who join you on your break who do not understand your language, speak in the language that everyone understands. This is simply being respectful.

Let your co-workers know ahead of time, that you need some downtime and it is more relaxing to speak in your first language during breaks.

> **Do not exclude others.**
>
> **Avoid speaking in your first language when working. Co-workers who do not speak your language often perceive it negatively.**

Learning to Understand other Cultures

Culture is much more than food, dance, song and traditions. Our cultures are formed by our values and beliefs.

There are steps you can take to learn about the cultural differences. The first step is to be aware of your own values, beliefs, assumptions, prejudices and stereotypes. How do each of these affect how you behave and what you think is right or wrong?

The next step is to try to understand the people who you are interacting with and their values, beliefs, assumptions, prejudices and stereotypes. How do each of these affect how they behave and what they think is right or wrong?

Ask questions of others to try to increase your understanding of their culture. Share information about your culture with others.

While you are learning about different cultures in the workplace, watch and observe. Ask questions and mimic others.

> **Always check your assumptions!**

Discrimination and Racism

In Canada, there are human rights laws to address discrimination and racism and a constitutional guarantee of equal rights for all. If you experience racism or discrimination in the workplace, most workplaces have respectful workplace policies and procedures to deal with such behaviours. Each province also has a Human Rights Commission where you can file a report if you are discriminated against.

There are seven discriminatory practices prohibited by the Canadian Human Rights Act[49]:

- "Denying someone goods, services, facilities or accommodation.
- Providing someone goods, services, facilities or accommodation in a way that treats them adversely and differently.
- Refusing to employ or continue to employ someone, or treating him or her unfairly in the workplace.
- Following policies or practices that deprive people of employment opportunities.
- Paying men and women differently when they are doing

---

[49] Canadian Human Rights Act, http://www.chrc-ccdp.ca/eng/content/what-discrimination

work of the same value.
- Retaliating against a person who has filed a complaint with the Commission or against someone who has filed a complaint for them.
- Harassing someone."

Regardless of the law, you are bound to experience racism and discrimination in your daily lives. You may face greater surveillance by the police. You may earn less income, regardless of your education and experience. You may overhear people making comments about what you wear, particularly for women. You may hear comments about being Muslim. This can be very stressful!

Try not to become depressed, bitter, angry or hurt. The best way to deal with racism and discrimination is to report it to your employer.

If you are confronted with discrimination or racism in your daily personal life, do not confront the person with anger. If you have a relationship with whoever is making the comment, then try to educate. If it is a stranger, you can either ignore the comment or politely reply. If it is an authority figure such as a police officer, then remain calm, do as you are told and then afterwards, report the incident to the Police Chief.

The best way to confront racism is to get involved in community activities that educate others about discrimination and racism. You will have a much better and broader impact. It is a way of turning something negative into something positive.

In Conclusion

Settlement assistance is available to you. Language training is available to you. Use both these opportunities to help you learn English or French and to settle successfully in Canada.

Integration is a process that will take many years to achieve. Ask questions when you do not understand something or are unsure of how to proceed. Get help when you are feeling depressed or sad or isolated.

Spend time with your family doing things that you enjoy. Spend time with other people from your home country. Spend time with people in your religious communities. Spend time becoming friends with people who are Canadian-born. Be active.

Check your assumptions. What you perceive may be an incorrect assumption as you are in a new country and a new culture.

Remember that everyone has an accent. Remember why you chose to come to Canada. Remember that Canada wants you to feel welcome.

Be patient! Do not give up!

Diversity ERAA Training wishes you well on your immigration journey in Canada!

APPENDICES

Appendix 1: Common Idioms and Terms

Terms and Idioms	Definition
Across the board	Something is applied to everyone equally
Actions speak louder than words	What a person actually does rather than what they say they will do
ASAP	As soon as possible
At the eleventh hour	Handing in assignments at the last minute
Biffy	Toilet
Bunnyhug (Saskatchewan)	Hooded pullover sweatshirt
Chesterfield	Sofa
Double-Double	A cup of coffee with two creams and two sugars
Downhomer	A resident of Newfoundland
Eh?	An interjection, similar to "you know?"
Face the music	Accept the consequences of your actions
Flea market	Outdoor shopping bazaar
FYI	For your information
Gameplan	Plan of action and a strategy to achieve goal
Give me a break	Give someone a chance
Grab a bite	Going to a restaurant to eat
Housecoat	Bathrobe
Hydro	Electricity
Icing on the cake	An extra bonus
I'm all ears	I am ready to listen
Islander	A person from Prince Edward Island
Jam buster (Manitoba)	Jelly doughnut
Keep your shirt on	Remain calm
Learn the ropes	Master the job
Long shot	Probability is small
Maritimer	A resident of the Maritime provinces

121

Term and Idioms	Definition
My lips are sealed	Will keep a secret and never tell
Mounties	Royal Canadian Mounted Police (RCMP)
Neck of the woods	A specific neighborhood or area where people live and common with
Nip in the bud	Stop a problem in the early stage
No strings attached	Do not have any obligations
On a shoestring	Living on very little money
Paint the town red	Going out and enjoying a night of entertainment
Part ways	Finished with a relationship either at work or personally
Pogie	Welfare; government assistance
Politically correct	Challenges vocabulary that implies prejudice, racism, sexism, homophobia
Pop	Bubbly soft drinks
Pulling your leg	Teasing or joking
Put it in a nutshell	Summarize it clearly
Raining cats and dogs	Very heavy rainfall
Red tape	Government bureaucracies that are time-consuming
R&R	Rest and relaxation
ROI	Return on investment
Rule of thumb	General guideline based on experience
Runners	Running shoes
Serviette	Napkin
Sneakers	Running shoes
Speak of the devil	Someone suddenly appear that you were discussing

Term and Idioms	Definition
Street dog (Toronto)	A hotdog in a bun sold by a street vendor
Take the ball and run	Move forward on an idea or new direction
Top brass	Most important senior people in an organization
Two-four	A 24-pack of beer
Walk in the park	Task or activity that is easy
Warts and all	Accepting a person's flaws
Water under the bridge	Put matter in the past

Common Jargon in Newfoundland and Labrador	Definition
Angishore	A weak, miserable person
Arn	Any
Bayman	Anyone not from St. John's
Bliver	To shiver with cold
Chucklehead	A stupid person
Clobber	An untidy state of things
Do you want some taken up	Want some supper
Duckish	Between sunset and dark
Gandy	Pancake
I just dies at you	You make me laugh
It's a mausey day	A foggy, wet day
Mind now	You do not really expect that
Mush	Porridge
Narn	None
Prog	Food
Stunned	Foolish or naive
Where's ya longs to	Where do you come from
Yer	Here
Yes b'y	Many meanings: I don't believe you; really it is true

Appendix 2: Sample Cover Letters

Job: Administrative

NAME

Street Address, City, Province, Postal Code

• Telephone Number   • Email address

Date

Person's Name of who cover letter should be sent
Title
Organization's Name
Street Address
City, Province, Postal Code

RE: Job Posting Title, Advertisement Number if stated

Dear Sir or Madam,

I am applying for the Administrative Officer for *Company Name*. I am extremely interested in this position as it perfectly fits my experience. For the past ten years, I have provided office management, and financial and administrative services to various organizations. As you can see in the chart below, my education and work experience qualifies me for the Administrative Officer position.

Job Requirements	My Qualifications
Must be legally entitled to work in Canada.	I am a Permanent Resident qualified to work in Canada.

Valid full class 5 Manitoba driver's license	I have a valid full class 5 Manitoba drier's license.
Experience in administrative and office management	As an Operations Manager in my current position, I oversee all business and highly confidential company matters including human resource management, vendor identification, procurement and management, facilities management, product purchasing and insurance, SEO, advertising, financial and accounting matters and legal compliance. This demonstrates my experience in administrative and office management.
Experience in managing staff and coordinating work	I currently supervise and coordinate the work of over 40 employees for 4 companies at 2 different locations. This includes supervising managers, accounting, service and sales staff.
Experience monitoring, preparing, coordinating, and maintaining financial information, including operational budgets, forecasting, variance reporting, and coding of payables	I currently forecast, prepare and monitor the budgets of 3 companies. I have reviewed and authorized over 2000 new loan applications for the purchase of vehicles, audited over 4000 sale files to ensure correct documentation and investigated audit defects.
Ability to develop and implement efficient administrative processes	I develop, implement and ensure compliance with administrative processes for my current employer including all **HR** policies and procedures.

Experience working with electronic accounting/financial software	I have experience using Simply Accounting and am able to learn new software applications relatively quickly.
Excellent verbal and written communication skills as well as strong interpersonal and customer service skills	I have demonstrated my strong communication skills, both verbal and written, throughout my career. In my various roles, I regularly liaised with customers, co-workers and vendors.

Verbal: In my current role, I handle all matters pertaining to the Better Business Bureau and Consumer Protection Office from customer complaints to release of documents. This role requires strong diplomacy and an ability to communicate common goals to diverse individuals and organizations.

Written: An example of my written communication skills in one of my roles was to prepare over 500 documents of transfer, 100 legal documents and 150 proof of claims for bankruptcies.

Interpersonal: I currently arrange and coordinate corporate events for customers and staff. Using my planning and organizational skills, I design the event, book space and interact with vendors. During the event, I interact with customers on a one-to-one basis. |

Excellent verbal and written communication skills as well as strong interpersonal and customer service skills	Customer Service: I have worked as frontline staff where I greeted and directed about 100 people per day. Currently, I resolve customer issues ensuring that their needs are met.
Strong problem solving skills	Problem solving is one of my strengths and I use this skill daily. I report directly to the company's President and am the primary decision-maker for operational matters. This includes resolving problems managers face with staff and customers, handling computer software issues and dealing with vendor concerns. One of my primary goals and expertise is to resolve problems so that the needs of the company are met while at the same time ensuring that an effective resolution is found for staff, customers and vendors.
Ability to prioritize a high volume of workload to meet deadlines with accuracy and strict attention to detail	Working in a fast-paced environment, with a multitude of diverse responsibilities, it is imperative that I am able to meet deadlines with accuracy and provide accurate details. For each step of the purchase of the product, I conduct the advertising, review loan application and legal documentation, monitor the budget inventory, plan sales events and arrange facilities, each of which must be met on a schedule.

Supervisory experience in a unionized environment	Although I have no direct experience supervising in a unionized environment, I know that successful labour relations starts with establishing good relationships with employees. From my current experience supervising staff, developing good communications with employees is an important step in developing trust and respect, which leads the way to successful labour relations.

I look forward to being interviewed where I can share my experience, strengths and abilities in more detail.

Thanks you for your consideration.

Yours sincerely,
Signature

Name

> Job: Finance

NAME
Street Address, City, Province, Postal Code
- Telephone Number
- Email address

Date

Person's Name of who cover letter should be sent
Title
Organization's Name
Street Address
City, Province, Postal Code

RE: Job Posting Title, Advertisement Number if stated

Dear Sir or Madam,

Twenty-one years experience in accounting and finance with a proven track record in managing the general ledger and financial reporting, administering accounting systems, developing annual budgets and forecasting, while building and maintaining positive relationships with internal and external clients, are just part of the knowledge I would bring to your position of Manager of Finance. I am a goal-oriented, self-starter who began as a volunteer in a similar non-profit community service society and within five months was employed in the accounting department of that same agency.

My extensive knowledge of accounting systems is important because I can spearhead the implementation of these systems to save money and improve accuracy. One of my recent accomplishments included initiating a comprehensive income and expense analysis that proved for early identification and correction of a posting error reducing 20% of month-end time and improving accuracy by 90%. Additionally, when I was preparing tax rebate applications, I noticed $120,000 of missing money owed to the agency. I also developed complex financial reports for forecasting, trending and results analysis that tracked lost money and showed proper invoicing.

During the course of my career, I have gained a specialist's understanding of financial instruments and accounting software and have also been effective in explaining complex information in a comprehensible manner. I am relied upon to convey essential financial data to all levels of management and external stakeholders, including advice on the auditing processes. I liaise with federal and provincial governments and 20 community agencies on financial and administrative functions and concerns, billing matters and contract changes. These include some of the same funders and partners as your organization, such as Citizenship and Immigration Canada, Ministry of Children and Family Services and the United Way, making me familiar with budget processes, grant applications, monitoring and reporting policies and procedures. My ability to be an effective communicator in dealing with staff, management and external funders, vendors and partners is the strength of my financial leadership.

My analytic, time-management and communication skills are excellent allowing me to meet cyclical deadlines and manage the numerous duties of the Manager of Finance with ease. I am meticulous when it comes to details and rarely make an accounting error.

My key accounting and financial competencies include, but are not limited to, bookkeeping, payroll, deferred revenue and accounts receivable schedules, account reconciliation, cash flow, preparation of accounting and financial reports and statements, budget monitoring systems maintenance, resource and expense tracking systems, resolution of any escalated vendor disputes and billing charges, monitoring and analysis of general ledger account and preparation of annual audit documentation, and provision of financial support. Currently, I train, lead and oversee the work of a 3-person accounting team and coordinate pay and benefits information flow to 80 employees. I have worked closely with all managers, in particular the Director of Human Resources, and am familiar with human resource policies and practices.

My experience and skills will enable me to make a valuable contribution to *Name of Organization* as Manager of Finance, and it would also be gratifying to be able to support and be part of an organization that promotes excellence and creates a culture of continuous improvement within business functions and program areas.

I will bring not only my years of expert experience but also my personal drive for results and positive outcomes. I am prepared for the next challenge in my career and look forward to an interview to discuss my qualifications more fully.

Sincerely,
Signature

Name

> Job: Hospitality Industry

NAME
Street Address, City, Province, Postal Code
- Telephone Number
- Email address

Date

Person's Name of who cover letter should be sent
Title
Organization's Name
Street Address
City, Province, Postal Code

RE: Job Posting Title, Advertisement Number if stated

Dear (Insert Mr. or Ms. Last Name or Sir and/or Madam):

As a seasoned, 10-year hospitality management professional with a proven track record of overseeing operations of 6 dining outlets with a 350-seat capacity in a 5-Star luxury 218-room hotel that serves 369,000 annually, this is what I would offer your hotel. I have experience working in the hotel industry under three different international hospitality brands, *LIST BRANDS* and have been promoted and consistently entrusted with large operational agendas throughout my employment. Currently, I lead a combined staff of 90, which also encompasses hiring, staff training, career coaching, scheduling, mentoring and evaluation. I strongly believe that my professional experience, educational background and track record align with the qualities and capabilities of the individual you are seeking to lead your operations to superior financial performance and exceptional guest satisfaction.

I have a Master's degree in Tourism Management with proven experience in hotel food and beverage operation management, customer service and team management. For the and past 6 years, I have been the Assistant Food and Beverages Manager at the *Name Hotel*. I am results-oriented with strong leadership and interpersonal skills, effective organizational and planning skills, exceptional customer service skills and excellent budgetary, projection and cost control skills ensuring the highest level of guest satisfaction at all times.

I have very strong verbal skills with the ability to communication effectively with staff members, executives, guests and vendors. I have strong problem solving skills and the ability to make good decisions while working under pressure in a fast-paced hotel environment while exceeding guest and company expectations. I always maintain a positive and friendly attitude. I have the ability to find solutions to problems and to resolve any issues arising with guests in a fast and efficient manner.

I have demonstrated skills and capabilities in:
- Managing day to day operations of all Food and Beverage outlets to deliver an excellent guest and team member experience
- Planning and controlling all areas of cost management pertaining to cost of food, beverages and other related expenses
- Planning and managing procurement, production and presentation of all food and beverages in the hotel in a safe, sanitary and cost effective manner to achieve a profitable result
- Ensuring that each customer receives outstanding service by providing a friendly and welcoming atmosphere
- Reviewing food service trends and suggesting modifications in menu and presentation
- Controlling food waste, product inventory, payroll and expenses

- Hiring, training, scheduling, supervising, motivating and evaluating staff
- Setting achievable goals, developing budgets, and monitoring revenues and expenditures
- Ensuring practice of health and safety regulations
- Ensuring compliance with all health and safety regulations and Company policies and procedures
- Acting as Hotel Manager once per month

My resume is attached which will provide you with more information about my skills and experience. I am confident that I will be an asset to your organization and look forward to working for you.

Thank you for taking the time to consider my application. I look forward to learning about the next steps in the selection process and can assure you that my drive, commitment and enthusiasm will be a great value to your team.

Sincerely,
Signature

Name

Appendix 3: Sample Resumes

> Job: Administrative Officer

NAME
Street Address, City, Province, Postal Code
- Telephone Number
- Email address

CAREER OBJECTIVE: Management Position

SUMMARY OF QUALIFICATIONS

Versatile, confident and organized Operations Manager with over 10 years of administrative experience. High level of professionalism with ability to hand confidential information and act with discretion. Ability to work in a team environment and independently with little or no supervision. Strong interpersonal, time management and communication skills with the ability to take initiative. Sound judgment and problem solving skills with the ability to handle sensitive and non-routine issues in a high paced environment. Experienced with diverse clientele.

PROFESSIONAL EXPERIENCE

JOB TITLE   **2011 - present**
COMPANY NAME, CITY, PROVINCE, COUNTRY (If outside Canada)

- Oversee all business and highly confidential company matters including human resource management, vendor identification, procurement and management, facilities management, product purchasing and insurance, SEO, advertising, financial and accounting matters and legal compliance

- Supervise over 40 employees working at four different companies and two locations
- Prepare and monitor account balances of three sister companies: *List 3 companies*
- Create and place 7 advertisements per day, handle 5-10 invoices per day and keep record of all pre-authorized payments
- Handle all matters pertaining to the Better Business Bureau and Consumer Protection office including customer complaints and release of relevant documents
- Purchased to date over 2000 vehicles on line at various auctions
- Organize all off-site sales including the organization of the sale facility, maintain Dealer Plates and secure all sales deposits in amounts ranging from $1000 to $200,000
- Developed, implemented and ensure compliance with company HR policies and procedures
- Reviewed and authorized to date over 2000 new loan applications and am Commissioner for Oaths
- Audited over 4000 files to ensure correct documentation and investigated audit defects
- Investigated and negotiated insurance claims and opened over 400 arbitration files
- Handled 7 Employment Standard cases and providing needed documents to authorities successfully achieving no penalties by the Employment Standards Branch
- Arranged and coordinated approximately 15 corporate events for staff and customers

JOB TITLE   **2010 - 2011**
COMPANY NAME, CITY, PROVINCE, COUNTRY (If outside Canada)

- Updated over 2500 conformation statements on Personal Property Registration

- Updated over 4000 credit reports to Trans Union of Canada and Equifax
- Prepared over 500 documents of transfer, 100 legal documents and 150 proof of claims for bankruptcies
- Performed clerical and administrative duties for Manager in sister company

JOB TITLE 2007 - 2010
COMPANY NAME, CITY, PROVINCE, COUNTRY (If outside Canada)

- Performed clerical duties including frontline reception
- Answered over 200 telephone calls per day from public
- Maintained records of daily attendance for 43 employees
- Greeted approximately 100 people daily and booked 5-10 daily appointments with clients
- Maintained inventory and ordered supplies form about 15 vendors

JOB TITLE 2011 - present
COMPANY NAME, CITY, PROVINCE, COUNTRY (If outside Canada)

- Provided support to 11-member sales team ensuring all sales and service objectives were met
- Maintained records of all orders, prepared invoices and prepared payment cheques
- Performed clerical duties including answering customer inquiries, problem solving, provision of new product information, training of new customer service representatives and development of new policies and procedures

LANGUAGES

Fluent in English, Hindi and Punjabi

COMPUTER SKILLS

Proficient in Microsoft Office Suite, Simply Accounting, database applications, electronic mail and Internet research
Keyboarding speed: 50 w.p.m.

EDUCATION

Masters Program in Business Administration, *Institution Name, Country, Year*
Bachelor of Arts (Accounting), *Institution Name, Country, Year*

PROFESSIONAL DEVELOPMENT

Training in WHMIS, Emergency First Aid and CPR

REFERENCES AVAILABLE ON REQUEST

Job: Finance

NAME
Street Address, City, Province, Postal Code
- Telephone Number
- Email address

SUMMARY OF QUALIFICATIONS

Twenty-one years of proven accounting management experience that emphasizes high productivity, efficiency, accuracy, ease-of-use and cost containment. Well-developed organizational, time management, communication and analytical skills with demonstrated problem-solving capabilities. Proven track record in achieving sound development and monitoring of budgets for grants, contracts and general funds. Familiar with a variety of accounting, finance, payroll and human resources concepts, practices and procedures. Self-motivating with the initiative and ability to multitask in a fast-paced environment with proven ability to work effectively to achieve agency objectives. Demonstrated experience working in a non-profit, unionized environment with the ability to work independently and as part of a team.

PROFESSIONAL EXPERIENCE

JOB TITLE   **1994 - present**
COMPANY NAME, CITY, PROVINCE, COUNTRY (If outside Canada)

Finance and Accounting

- Direct and control the operations of the accounting function and financial activities of *Name of Organization* including bookkeeping, payroll, deferred revenue and accounts receivable schedules, account reconciliation, cash flow, preparation of accounting and financial, narrative and statistical reports and statements, budget monitoring systems maintenance, resource

and expense tracking systems, resolution of any escalated vendor disputes and billing charges, monitoring and analysis of general ledger account, preparation of annual audit documentation, and provision of financial support to directors and managers
- Develop and coordinate annual $10,000,000 budget preparation in conjunction with 18 managers and 8 program directors providing on-going financial information/recommendations throughout the fiscal year
- Contribute to and review 22 funding proposals and applications annually
- Analyze 13 project reports monthly and contributions/grant details, provide accurate financial information and advice to 9 program managers, process 13 monthly and 7 quarterly claims to funders, coordinate approval processes of 140 accounts payable invoices per month, rectify escalated accounts payable issues monthly from 10 employees and 5 vendors, code the general ledger and process vendor invoice payments ranging from $120 to $55,000
- Perform accurate billings and monthly posting to remediation accounts for $25,000 budget, deposit third party cheques of $500,000/month and monthly reserve transfers of $24,000, handle month end allocations including opening approximately 10 new accounts monthly, and conduct month-end balance sheet reviews, reconcile any variances and prepare month end financial statements for directors
- Coded the general ledger and processed 120 vendor invoice payments of $55,000

Supervisory Skills and Human Resources

- Train, coach, mentor and lead the work of a 3-person team
- Coordinate information flow regarding pay and benefits to 80 employees

- Maintain up-to-date knowledge and understanding of ever changing HR requirements, policies and procedures, labour standard laws and collective agreement
- Recommend corrective actions on accounting issues to Senior Managers
- Recruit and interview potential candidates for available accounting positions

Internal and External Client Engagement

- Clarify, coach and guide 8 directors and 18 managers on budgeting, invoicing, monthly financial updates and periodic financial reporting tasks
- Meet with 6 Department Heads to communicate financial information as needed
- Collaborate with 26 directors and managers to reconcile accounts ranging from $5,000 to $4,500,000
- Liaise with federal and provincial governments and 20 community agencies including *Name Agencies* on matters related to financial and administrative functions and concerns, billing matters and contract changes
- Produce and release financial information to 9 different funding agencies, 12 other organizations, and 22 external auditors

Facilities and Equipment Monitoring

- Monitor purchase of all agency capital assets totaling $75,000 and oversee assignment of assets to departments
- Monitor all leased equipment contract payments totaling $25,000 and balance and designate the fees according to program usage

Information Systems Management

- Implemented an information system, in conjunction with *Job Title* Interpretation Translation department, that was to be used on an interim basis prior to software purchase but remains in use till date due to its efficiency and effectiveness

Risk Prevention, Management and Accreditation

- Prepared all documentation for *Name Organization's* agency accreditation in conjunction with the Executive Director and accounting team
- Participate in on-going risk prevention and management activities

COMPUTER SKILLS

Proficient in Accounting and Payroll software including AccPac-Sage, Pay@Work-ADP, ERP, and Simply accounting and Microsoft Office applications Access, Excel, Outlook, PowerPoint, Word and Windows XP Professional OS

LANGUAGES

Fluent in English and Spanish

EDUCATION

Diploma in computerized Accounting, *Institution Name, Country, Year*
Faculty of Business Administration, *Institution Name, Country, Year*

PROFESSIONAL DEVELOPMENT

Conflict Resolution Workshop, 2015
CIC Regulations and Ways to Make Proper Claims Webinar, 2014
Year-End Payroll Workshop, 2012
Government Changes Workshop, 2004
Communication Workshop, 2003
Year-End Payroll Workshop, 1994

REFERENCES UPON REQUEST

Job: Hospitality Industry

NAME
Street Address, City, Province, Postal Code
- Telephone Number
- Email address

CAREER OBJECTIVE: FOOD AND BEVERAGE MANAGER

SUMMARY OF QUALIFICATIONS

Proven manager with over seventeen years of hospitality experience in hotel food and beverage operation management, customer service and team management. Results-oriented with strong leadership and interpersonal skills; effective organizational, planning and communication skills; exceptional customer service skills; and excellent budgetary, projection and cost control skills ensuring the highest level of guest satisfaction at all times. Demonstrated ability to work under pressure in a fast-pace hotel environment while exceeding guest and company expectations. Self-motivating with the initiative and ability to multitask and oversee, supervise and train 90 staff in multiple hotel dining outlets.

PROFESSIONAL EXPERIENCE

JOB TITLE   **2012 - present**
COMPANY NAME, CITY, PROVINCE, COUNTRY (If outside Canada)

- Direct and oversee operations of 6 dining outlets with 350-seat capacity in 218-room 5 Star hotel forecasted to annually serve 369,000
- Hire, train, schedule, supervise, motivate, evaluate and lead team of 90 staff to maximize employee engagement, service and teamwork

- SMART START Develop and sustain personal contact with culinary team and in-room dining team to maintain high quality food and beverage offerings and impeccable presentation in line with hotel standards.
- Lead, guide and direct operations of each dining facility to maximize profitability and minimize operating costs
- Plan, direct and implement Food and Beverage strategic business plans •
- Prepare and monitor the annual Food and Beverage budgets and revenue forecasts pro-actively addressing trough periods•
- Analyze Profit and Loss statements and develop strategies for improvement and guest experience enhancements•
- Participate actively in the hotel community to further inter-departmental working relationships
- Acts as Hotel General Manager once per month demonstrating ability to apply technical, professional or product expertise to everyday hotel situations

JOB TITLE 2010 - 2012
COMPANY NAME, CITY, PROVINCE, COUNTRY (If outside Canada)

- Directed and oversaw operations of 150-seat capacity restaurant leading 28-member team
- Responsible for all revenues, expenditures and annual budget
- Introduced a minimum of one touch-point per quarter.
- Managed customer database to effectively market and promote restaurant products and services.
- Established guest service standards and monitored implementation to ensure target market needs were met.
- Conducted departmental orientation training for all new employees.

- Recruited prospective employees at Catering Colleges as part of hotel's recruitment strategy and interview panel member.

JOB TITLE   **2008 - 2010**
COMPANY NAME, CITY, PROVINCE, COUNTRY (If outside Canada)

- Directed and oversaw operations of 150-seat capacity restaurant leading 28-member team
- Improved guest satisfaction tracking system results from 76% to 89% consistently quarter to quarter during 2010-11

JOB TITLE   **2002 - 2008**
COMPANY NAME, CITY, PROVINCE, COUNTRY (If outside Canada)

- Directed and oversaw operations of 70-seat capacity lounge and bar leading a 8-member team
- Awarded *Best Manager* in 2009

LANGUAGES
Fluent in English and Hindi

COMPUTER SKILLS
Proficient in Windows, Triton, Opera and OnQ

EDUCATION
Masters in Tourism Management, *Institution Name, Country, Year*
Hotel Management Diploma, *Institution Name, Country, Year*

REFERENCE UPON REQUEST

Appendix 4: Sample Interview Questions and Answers

1. *Tell us about yourself.*

Answer: The response is job/career related not personal. Make sure you know your resume back to front - you may be asked about skills and experience from previous jobs, which may be more relevant for the role you are interviewing for.

You need to have a short statement prepared in your mind. Be careful that it does not sound rehearsed. Limit it to work-related items unless instructed otherwise. Talk about things you have done and jobs you have held that relate to the position you are interviewing for. Start with the item farthest back and work up to the present.

2. *What do you know about this company?*

Answer: Do as much research as you can about the company. What does it do/sell/make? How many employees work there? What is its mission and goals? Where does it operate? What are the current issues and who are the major players including competitors? You can insert how your skills and abilities will help the company in their goals and future. These are the key things you should know about a company before going to the interview.

Do the background work, it will make you stand out as someone who comes prepared, and is genuinely interested in the company and the job.

3. Why do you want to work for us?

Answer: Here is where you tell them what is great about their organization and link it to your career goals. Your answer should be directly related to the last question. Any research you've done on the company should have led you to the conclusion that you'd want to work there. Put some thought into this answer before you have your interview, mention your career goals and highlight forward-thinking goals and career plans. Do not talk about needing a job, being unemployed, the salary or benefits. Sincerity is extremely important here and will easily be sensed.

4. What experiences do you have in this field?

Answer: Speak about specifics that relate to the position you are applying for. If you do not have specific experience, get as close as you can.

5. In your last position, what were your most significant accomplishments?

Answer: Always mention a work-related achievement (heading up a successful project or saving the company money is always a good choice), and if you've run a marathon or scaled a mountain, that's an achievement that could be woven into the conversation too.

6. What are your greatest strengths?

Answer: Numerous answers are acceptable. Just stay positive. A few good examples: Your ability to prioritize, Your problem-solving skills, Your ability to work under pressure, Your ability to focus on projects, Your professional expertise, Your leadership skills, Your positive attitude, etc.

7. What is your biggest weakness?

Answer: Recognizing the areas in your character and working life that need to be improved is a sign to the interviewer that you are self-aware and strive to progress. If you're asked this question, give a small, work-related flaw that you're working hard to improve. Example: "I've been told I occasionally focus on details and miss the bigger picture, so I've been spending time laying out the complete project every day to see my overall progress."

8. How would your former boss and/or colleagues describe you?

Answer: This is another opportunity to be positive about yourself, so remember to reiterate all your good points especially as they relate to the position you are being interviewed for.

Be prepared with a quote or two from co-workers. Either a specific statement or a paraphrase will work, e.g., One of my co-workers always said I was the hardest worker she had ever known" or even better, "One of my co-workers has always said I was the most reliable, creative problem-solver he'd ever met."

9. Tell us about a problem you had with a supervisor.

Answer: This is a test to see if you will speak ill of your boss. If you fall for it and tell about a problem with a former boss, you may well blow the interview right there. Stay positive and develop a poor memory about any trouble with a supervisor.

10. Describe how you are a team player?

Answer: Be sure to have examples ready. Specifics that show you often perform for the good of the team rather than for yourself are good evidence of your team attitude. Do not brag; just say it in a matter-of-fact tone. This is a key point.

11. Describe a situation where you have ... and how you handled it:

- *Usually these items are taken from the job ad*
- **Example:** *worked under pressure*

Answer: You may say that you thrive under certain types of pressure. Give an example that relates to the type of position applied for.

12. What motivates you to do your best on the job?

Answer: This is a personal trait that only you can say, but good examples are: Challenge, Achievement, and Recognition

13. What qualities do you look for in a boss?

Answer: Be generic and positive. Safe qualities are knowledgeable, a sense of humour, open to new ideas, fair and supportive.

14. What are your goals for the future?

Answer: Employers want to be sure that you won't be moving on to another job right away. The best way to respond to the interview question "What are your goals for the future?" or "Where do you see yourself in five years?" is to refer to the position and the company you are interviewing with. Connect your answer to the job you are applying for. For example, "My long-term goals involve growing with a company where I can continue to learn, take on additional responsibilities and contribute as much value as I can."

15. Why should we hire you?

Answer: Highlight your best points as they relate to the position being discussed. Give a little advance thought to this relationship. Point out how your assets meet what the organization needs. Do not mention any other candidates to make a comparison.

16. What salary do you expect/need?

Answer: Do not answer it as you have already stated this in your cover letter. Instead, say something like, "Can you tell me the range for this position?" In most cases, the interviewer, taken off guard, will tell you. If not, say what you wrote in the cover letter.

17. Any questions for us?

Answer: Remember an interview is a two-way conversation; so be prepared to ask relevant questions. There's no need to wait until the end, feel free to interject with queries and comments as the conversation flows. This will not only give you relevant insight into the organization, it will also help you engage with the interviewer and show that you are confident individual who listens and interacts.

You can show your enthusiasm and interest by discussing aspects of the training programs or talking about the working culture or opportunities for gaining further qualifications. You can ask what a typical career path for someone with your skills and experiences are within the company.

Alternatively, if the interview does not give an opportunity to discuss an aspect of your course, work or extracurricular activities that you feel strongly supports your application, this is an appropriate time to mention it (briefly!).

Bibliography

Banks Operating in Canada, Canadian Bankers Association, www.cba.ca/en/component/content/category/61-banks-operating-in-canada

Calgary Economic Development, http://www.calgaryeconomicdevelopment.com/industries

Canadian Immigrants, http://www.canadaimmigrants.com/immigration/statistics/

Canadian Association of Statutory Human Rights Agencies, Links, www.cashra.ca/links.html

Canadian Human Rights Act, http://www.chrc-ccdp.ca/eng/content/what-discrimination

Caring for Kids New to Canada, Canadian Paediatric Society, www.kidsnewtocanada.ca/mental-health/ptsd

Central Intelligence Agency, https://www.cia.gov

City Data, http://www.city-data.com/canada/Winnipeg-work.html

City of Fredericton, http://www.fredericton.ca/en/communityculture/communityprofile.asp

City of Ottawa, *Economy and Demographics*, http://ottawa.ca/en/long-range-financial-plans/long-range-financial-plan-iii-part-1-and-part-2/economy-and-demographics

City of Toronto, *Key Industry Sectors*, http://www1.toronto.ca/wps/portal/contentonly?vgnextoid=401132d0b6d1e310VgnVCM10000071d60f89RCRD

Constructive Criticism, Wikipedia, https://en.wikipedia.org/wiki/Constructive_criticism

Economic Development Brandon, http://economicdevelopmentbrandon.com/industry-employment-business

eMentalHealth.ca, http://m.ementalhealth.ca/index.php?m=article&ID=8885&r=Winnipeg-Regional-Health-Authority

Employment and Social Development Canada, http://srv129.services.gc.ca/ei_regions/eng/vancouv.aspx?rates=1

Employment and Social Development Canada, http://srv129.services.gc.ca/ei_regions/eng/edmonton.aspx?rates=1

Employment and Social Development Canada, http://srv129.services.gc.ca/ei_regions/eng/calgary.aspx?rates=1

Employment and Social Development Canada, http://srv129.services.gc.ca/ei_regions/eng/winnipeg.aspx?rates=1

Employment and Social Development Canada, http://srv129.services.gc.ca/ei_regions/eng/toronto.aspx?rates=1

Expatistan, *Cost of Living Index*, www.expatistan.com

Found Locally, http://foundlocally.com/stjohns/Local/Info-CityInfo.htm

Government of Canada, *Labour Laws*: http://www.labour.gc.ca/eng/home.shtml

HeretoHelp, BC Partners for Mental Health and Addictions Information, http://www.heretohelp.bc.ca/visions/trauma-and-victimization-vol3/war-trauma-in-refugees

Housing in Canada, Citizenship and Immigration Canada, www.cic.gc.ca/english/newcomers/after-housing.asp

Immigration and Ethnocultural Diversity in Canada, Statistics Canada, www12.statcan.gc.ca/nhs-enm/2011/as-sa/99-010-x/99-010-x2011001-eng.cfm

Labour Force Characteristics, Population 15 and Older, by Census Metropolitan, Statistics Canada, www.statcan.gc.ca/tables-tableaux/sum- som/l01/cst01/labor35-eng.htm

Labour Force Characteristics, Unadjusted, by Census Metropolitan, Statistics Canada, www.statcan.gc.ca/tables-tableaux/sum-som/l01/cst01/lfss04k- eng.htm

Living in Canada, living in New Brunswick, http://www.livingin-canada.com/living-in-new-brunswick.html

MoneySense, http://www.moneysense.ca/canadas-best-places-to-live-2015-full-ranking/

National Average Price Map, The Canadian Real Estate Association, http://crea.ca/content/national-average-price-map

Office of the Superintendent of Financial Institutions, May 2014, http://www.osfi-bsif.gc.ca/eng/pages/default.aspx

Population of Census Metropolitan Areas, Statistics Canada, www.statcan.gc.ca/tables-tableaux/sum-som/l01/cst01/demo05a-eng.htm

Population Density, The World Bank, http://data.worldbank.org/indicator/EN.POP.DNST
Provincial Workplace Standards:
www.esdc.gc.ca/en/jobs/workplace/index.page

Quebec International, http://www.quebecinternational.ca/key-industries

Sirin, Selcuk R. and Rogers-Sirin, Lauren, *The Educational and Mental Health Needs of Syrian Refugee Children*, Migration Policy Institute, October 2015

Statistics Canada, http://www12.statcan.gc.ca/nhs-enm/2011/as-sa/99-010-x/99-010-x2011001-eng.cfm

Statistics Canada, *Immigration and Ethnocultural Diversity in Canada*, http://www12.statcan.gc.ca/nhs-enm/2011/as-sa/99-010-x/99-010-x2011001-eng.cfm

Statistics Canada, *Labour Force Characteristics, Unemployment*, http://www5.statcan.gc.ca/cansim/a26?lang=eng&retrLang=eng&id=2820135&paSer=&pattern=&stByVal=1&p1=1&p2=37&tabMode=dataTable&csid

Statistics Canada, *Life Satisfaction Across Metropolitan Areas and Economic Regions in Canada*, http://www.statcan.gc.ca/pub/11-626-x/11-626-x2015046-eng.htm

Statistics Canada, *Median Total Income, by Family Type, By Census Metropolitan Areas*, http://www.statcan.gc.ca/tables-tableaux/sum-som/l01/cst01/famil107a-eng.htm

Statistics Canada, *Population of Census Metropolitan Areas*, http://www.statcan.gc.ca/tables-tableaux/sum-som/l01/cst01/demo05a-eng.htm

The Canadian Real Estate Association, *National Average Price Map*, http://crea.ca/content/national-average-price-map

The Canadian Trade Commissioner Service, *St. John's: An Emerging Economy and Cultural Capital*, http://www.international.gc.ca/investors-investisseurs/cities-villes/saint_johns.aspx?lang=eng

The City of Edmonton, *Industries*, http://www.edmonton.ca/business_economy/demographics_profiles/industries.aspx

The Old Farmer's Almanac, http://www.almanac.com/content/windchill-chart-canada

The WorldBank, http://data.worldbank.org/indicator/SP.POP.TOTL

Two small men with big hearts, http://twosmallmen.com/halifax-ns-movers/main-industries-and-job-opportunities-in-halifax

World Fact Book, Central Intelligence Agency, www.cia.gov/library/publications/resources/the-world-factbook/

What are Bridging Programs for Internationally-Trained Professionals and Tradespeople, Settlement.Org, http://settlement.org/ontario/employment/plan-my-career/job-skills-training/what-are-bridging-programs-for-internationally-trained-professionals-and-tradespeople/

Wikipedia, https://en.wikipedia.org/wiki/Constructive_criticism

Wind Chill - The Chilling Facts, Environment Canada, www.ec.gc.ca/meteo-weather/default.asp?lang=En&n=5FBF816A-1#table1

Workers Rights in Canada, Service Canada, www.servicecanada.gc.ca/eng/about/publication/workers_rights.shtml

World Health Organization, www.emro.who.int/jor/jordan-news/syrian-refugees.html

Index

Appendices, 120
    Appendix 1: Common Idioms, 121
    Appendix 2: Sample Cover Letters, 124
    Appendix 3: Sample Resumes, 135
    Appendix 4: Sample Interview Questions and Answers, 146
Apply for Benefits, 48
Arrival, 1
Bibliography, 151
Buy a Computer or Laptop, 57
Buying Food and Household Goods, 51
Buy a Cell Phone (Mobile), 53
Canadian Laws, 34
    Drinking and Driving, 61
    Family Violence, 35
    Parking Tickets, 61
    Seat Belts and Child Safety Seats, 61
    Speeding, 62
    Texting and Hands Free Talking, 62
    Traffic Laws, 60
Checklists
    Finding a Job Checklist, 98
    Pre-Arrival Documentation Checklist, 39
    Rental Checklist, 56
    Settlement Checklist, 65
    Symptoms Checklist, 44
Credential Recognition for Regulated Professions, 57
Cultural Differences, 99
    Common Cultural Differences and Business Practices, 104
    Constructive Criticism, 110
    Cultural Quiz, 99
    Cultural Values and Beliefs, 102
    Expectations of Honesty, 112
    Food and Invitations, 114

    Informality, 108
    Learning to Understand other Cultures, 116
    LGBTT, 36
    Names, 114
    Perceptions and Assumptions, 102
    Politeness, 115
    Privacy and Personal Space, 109
    Punctuality, 107
    Relationships at Work, 112
    Showing Initiative, 111
    Socializing, 111
Discrimination and Racism, 117
Education, 31
    Attending College or University, 62
    Colleges, 63
    Choosing a Public School, 34
    Differences in Education, 33
    Register Your Children in School, 51
    Universities, 64
Employee Rights, 95
    Employment Standards, 95
    Human Rights, 96
    Workplace, Health and Safety, 96
Financial
    Banking, 23, 52
    Credit, 26
    Currency, 25
    Deductions from Your Paycheque, 94
    Other Deductions, 95
    Pensions, 94
    Taxes, 94
Find Childcare, 58
Finding a Job, 67, 77
    Alternative Career, 76
    Canadian Work Experience, 85

    Getting a License to Practice Your Profession, 67
    Elevator Pitch, 84
    How to Become a Successful Networker, 82
    Internships, 86
    Job Interview Preparation, 90
    Job Offer, 93
    Job Shadowing, 86
    Networking, 81
    Preparing to Find a Job, 67
    Resume (CV) Writing, 89
    Transferable Skills, 69
    Transferable Skills Inventory, 70
    Volunteering, 85
    Writing Cover Letters, 87

Health
    Find Medical Care, 54
    Health Insurance, 49
    Medical Emergencies, 50
    Post Traumatic Stress Disorder, 43

Housing, 26
    Find a Permanent Home, 55
    Garbage Collection and Littering, 29

In Conclusion, 118

Learn about Canada, 1
    Alberta, 3
    Atlantic Provinces, 9
    Canada's Prairie Provinces, 3
    Canada's West Coast Province, British Columbia, 1
    Canadian Cities Compared, 12
    Central Canada, 7
    Comparing Canada's Population and Age, 15
    Manitoba, 6
    New Brunswick, 9
    Newfoundland and Labrador, 11

      Northern Territories: Yukon, Northwest Territories And Nunavut, 12
      Nova Scotia, 10
      Official Languages, 22
      Ontario, 7
      Prince Edward Island, 11
      Quebec, 8
      Saskatchewan, 5

Mentorship, 86

Pre-Arrival, 1

Recreation and Leisure, 37

Settlement, 47

Settlement and Integration, 39
    Immigrant Settlement Services, 53
    Stages of Integration, 41

Social Insurance Number, 47

Take a Tour of Where You Live, 54

Transportation, 36
    Get a Driver's License, 58
    Purchasing Car Insurance, 59

Weather, 16
    Layer Your Clothes, 18
    Understand Wind Chill, 21

Workplace Communication Skills, 79
    Common Canadian Terms and Idioms, 80
    Eye Contact, 107
    Greetings, 105
    Leave Telephone Voice Messages, 109
    Speaking Your First Language at Work, 115
    Touching, 113

Your First Few Weeks, 54

Your First Week, 47

Your First Year, 58

About the Author

Barbara Dixon is the Senior Consultant and President of Diversity ERAA Training. She is recognized internationally as one of Canada's top diversity trainers and innovative leaders in immigrant integration programming. She has delivered workshops and keynote presentations to over 23,000 participants within 110 organizations across Canada and internationally. She is author of the *Newcomer's Guide to Canada*.

Barbara envisioned and created Canada's first post-secondary institution's diversity and immigrant student support department, initiated and implemented the first Certificate Program in Canada to train certified intercultural trainers, established the first Centre for Immigrant and International Students at a Canadian college and started the first Mentor Program for Immigrants in Canada before it was even called mentoring.

Barbara developed the pre-arrival group orientation workshop for the Canadian Immigrant Integration Program (CIIP) for Federal Skilled Workers and provincial nominees from Manitoba, Saskatchewan and the East Coast provinces. Currently, she is working on professionalizing Cultural Brokers. She has travelled to 27 countries and has worked in Nigeria, India, China, Philippines and the UK.

Barbara is available to help you settle and integrate successfully in Canada.

You can contact Barbara at: **diversityeraa@gmail.com** or **204-294-2234** or through the Diversity ERAA website: **http://diversityeraa.ca**